Thomas C. O'Donn

Life in a North Woods Lumber Camp

Edited and with Biographical
& Historical Commentary by

William J. O'Hern

Thomas C. O'Donnell's

Life in
a North Woods
Lumber Camp

Edited and with Biographical
& Historical Commentary by William J. O'Hern

Published by
The Forager Press, LLC
23 Bridge Street
Cleveland, NY 13042
www.TheForagerPress.com

Printed in the United States of America
by Versa Press, Inc.

ISBN 978-0-9743943-6-7

Also by
William J. O'Hern

Adirondack Adventures:
Bob Gillespie and Harvey Dunham
on French Louie's Trail
By Roy E. Reehil and William J. O'Hern
The Forager Press, LLC, 2012

Noah John Rondeau's
Adirondack Wilderness Days: A Year
with the hermit of Cold River Flow
The Forager Press, LLC, 2009

Under An Adirondack Influence:
The Life of A.L. Byron-Curtiss, 1871–1959
By Roy E. Reehil and William J. O'Hern
The Forager Press, LLC, 2008

Adirondack Characters
and Campfire Yarns: Early Settlers
and Their Traditions
The Forager Press, LLC, 2005

Adirondack Stories
of the Black River Country
North Country Books, Inc. 2003

Anyplace Wild in the Adirondacks
Self-published, 2000

Life with Noah:
Stories and Adventures of Richard Smith
With Noah J. Rondeau
North Country Books, Inc. 1997

In Appreciation

New York State regional author Thomas C. O'Donnell, formerly of Boonville, tapped upstate history for his four books published in the late 1940s and 1950s. His works are a gold mine of local lore, characters and funny stories—the kinds of books that you can read straight through without stopping, which is about the highest praise I can offer any writer.

During his retirement he began to develop a sixth book. It was to be his personal recollection of growing up in a family-owned logging camp. Mr. O'Donnell recorded stories of his father's lumber business and the hardships his mother faced living in the woods, and he wrote with nostalgia about his adventurous youth and how his brother and he mastered their ABC's in a backwoods log-cabin school house and lived as children did before the dawn of television. The tug of his boyhood years was strong, as evidenced by the reflective narratives left in O'Donnell's unpublished memoir.

I would like to acknowledge, posthumously, Thomas C. O'Donnell. Special recognition goes to grandson Thomas A. O'Donnell, who gave permission to reshape his grandfather's unfinished manuscript where needed, always with an eye to capturing Tom's distinctive voice, which is clearly evident in his uncompleted work.

Life in a North Woods Lumber Camp is much more than the history of the O'Donnell family business. Although the logging industry was a huge part of American history, to see it from such an up-close-and-personal perspective is both a privilege and a delight.

Table of Contents

Old-style Horse Logging

© R.P. Nadeau

LIFE IN A NORTH WOODS LUMBER CAMP

"TIM-BERRR!!" Can there be a more captivating expression in logging language, echoing through the forest? Probably not to the lumberjack. There are old-time "jacks" who found their experiences ideal, or at least unforgettable.

There were pain and glory, all-work-and-no-play, big sleigh-loads of logs, long hours of working with horses and mules, swinging double-bitted axes and drawing two-man crosscut handsaws from before daylight until dark. They devoured incredible quantities of lumber camp food, and took their pleasure in the raw, wild, and free-wheeling life of lumberjack towns.

Eventually, old-style loggers found themselves unable to load the huge softwoods on sleighs and leap sure-footed from one slippery log to another during log drives on rushing spring-swollen rivers. They were no longer quick enough to prepare a charge of dynamite to break up ice and blast troublesome rocks in a river to prevent log jams, or to side-step an unexpected black bear. Exposure to the unremitting raw, often sub-zero temperatures during long hours with a snow roller, or on a water tank crew icing the sleigh ruts, increased rheumatic pains. They experienced lame hands, legs, and feet and smarting muscle cramps after buzzing down trees all day with crosscut saws. Those who had accepted life in the lumber woods were forced to quit lumbering and take employment on the outside.

Despite the dangers and disadvantages of the old days of logging, there was a special pride in old-time know-how and hard work. And nothing could beat the shiver one got hearing the warning cry of "Tim-ber-r!!" just before a thundering virgin tree crashed to the ground, with echoes booming and trailing away off into the woods as a cloud of glistening soft powder snow rose and drifted gently back to earth. These were the things that fixed life in the logging camp in the hearts and minds of those who were willing to "tough 'er out" and accept life away from wives and children, home and farm—these and the need to earn money that could improve a family's life.

Venerable, robust, tough-as-nails, my 78-year-old pal, Leigh Portner, operates a one-man logging business, runs a time-worn sawmill, and as a practical aspect of the business, to be self-reliant, he repairs his own equipment and machinery. Leigh was enthusiastic when I shared my idea of relating the everyday drama of the lumberjack scene. "It wasn't no colorful life," he said. "How are you going to tell all the heck and high water lumbermen had to put up with?"

"Through dedication," I responded. "It will be a labor of love." There was a year in my life when I made my livelihood at Crockett's Saw Mill. I've known sawyers, yardmen, and graders, as well as those who worked in the woods. I was born too late to labor beside Redbeard Spike and Lars the Swede, big bruising Russians and Poles, or Frenchy from up Canada way—all of whom claimed they had been born with a pike pole in one hand and a canthook in the other. Yet, even in my younger years, I too felt the exhaustion of lumber work from my stint in the lumber industry. From personal experience (and being a bit of a recovering lumberjack-aholic) I have an understanding of the loggers' work and lifestyle and the importance they played in America's logging industry. I admire the old-time loggers. I told Leigh my intention was simply "to try," with his support.

For a historical record and from the standpoint of accuracy, *Life in a*

North Woods Lumber Camp tells a true life story while at the same time conveying general information about the occupational and social life of the men and women who worked in the timber woods, and the hardships and lumber-harvesting methods of the past, through the use of rare photographs snapped by photographers who followed the lumbermen and by principals who worked in the camps—reflected memories Leigh and I have gathered from dozens of former loggers we've sought out over the years.

Every former jack had a memorable experience to share. All graciously invited us into their homes to sit and listen, to ask questions, to videotape and tape record their personal experiences. All spoke of a demanding but fulfilling woods life. Due to injury, age, family obligations, or the need for a less rigorous job, they all had long ago left behind their logging lives for good. They now relax in comfortable retirement with memories of their long-ago lives in the woods. They tend their gardens and look at vintage snapshots taken when they earned their livelihoods cutting trees deep in the forests.

Tom O'Donnell's taste for life in a wilderness lumber camp clearly rushed through his mind first when Frank A. Reed, sky pilot and founder-editor-publisher of *The Lumber Camp News*, asked O'Donnell in January 1952 if he would take the leadership role to start a redesign of Reed's newspaper into a monthly magazine and to join *The Northeastern Logger* as an occasional writer and consultant.

O'Donnell's lumber camp interest continued as he learned more about the Adirondack land and natives—common people, mostly—about their ways and the drive and grit it took to make a living where the snow arrives in October and does not disappear until May—as he gathered research material for *Birth of a River*, his tenth work. The 1953 release documented the spirit of early North Country days in the Black River region of the Adirondack Mountains.

Mr. O'Donnell's son, Alfred C. O'Donnell, was co-editor of the *Boonville-Herald*. Father and son had discussions about how Tom's memories often matched those of Adirondack old-timers whose families opened the coun cleared the farms, built and tended reservoirs, owned and operated mills

and supplied neighboring urban centers with wood products. The picturesque country-side, the forests and rivers, and his parents' heyday of running a family lumbering industry full of colorful local characters

Thomas Clay O'Donnell was born July 29, 1881, in a lumber camp near Saginaw, Michigan to George and Vesta O'Donnell.

COURTESY OF CLIFFORD H. GILL FROM *THE MEMOIRS OF CLIFFORD H. GILL*

captured his imagination. Tom had written many imaginative and informal history books, but never one about his past.

Not wanting to lay aside the exciting adventure of his youth, he began a memoir—one that reads like a novel, but a funny novel, for O'Donnell is a master of understated humor—that went back to childhood. Tom explored his youthful hopes and the events in a home where "tote sleigh," "cruising timber," "woods horses," "road monkey," "pike pole" and "peavey" were household words.

For Tom, the writing was a glimpse back to moments of great pleasure, much as one glances back for another look at an appreciated picture in a gallery of art treasures. Unfortunately, circumstances never allowed him to see his final project through.

In both excited and quiet tones, Leigh and I enjoyed former lumbermen's tales of the sub-zero nights, the accidental death of a man who lost his life in the company's spring river drive, the crowded bunkhouses and lumber camp community, the legends, yarns and occasional practical joke. I sensed the former lumbermen found these memories more profitable to recall than their more recent work. Lamentable as the loss of their personal heritage was, their moribund culture may be just a metaphor for a more concrete decline: The timberlands were being taken over by machinery and new equipment that brought safer and less-expensive methods to harvest trees.

Bill Marleau, a forest ranger and friend, wrote in his book, *Big Moose Station*, about an Adirondack lumber camp in deep winter when the main haul roads were packed down and rolled and the surface iced with the use of a sprinkler wagon. This made it easier for the log-sleigh teams to move huge loads. Work was on a predawn to after-sunset timetable. *"Beautiful music could be heard on below-zero nights. The trees popping with frost, the squealing of sleigh runners on the frozen snow, the squeaking and jingling of the harness on the horse, their snorting with cold, the men stamping their feet and beating their hands together to keep warm, frozen words drifting out of the men's mouths off into the frigid night, the noise of pulp hitting pulp, could be heard for almost a mile on such a night."*

Marleau's words do not romanticize those sub-zero days and nights. Working loggers would never view their quality of life in that way. The freezing cold was real enough—it needed no embellishment.

Why try to tell today's people about logging days a century ago? No one works today as hard as loggers once did.

Precisely. Twenty-first century people are interested in early logging in the Adirondacks because of the hardiness of the men and the tough lives they led. My mission is to share what was going on before the days of widespread mechanization—when there was still a pioneer flavor in the isolated forest communities distant from the railroads, and the mills where the pine, spruce, white cedar, balsam fir, basswood and hemlock were taken. My mission was to undertake a project that shares the heartaches and the headaches, the thrill of the dangers they faced, and their simple pleasures.

By the close of the old-style logging era, the pine and hemlock were all but gone, and in place of the majestic softwoods there grew up areas covered with small, useless, low-growing plants like the wild cherry, poplar and several varieties of berry bushes, all mixed in with the debris of limbs and tops and butts of the toppled trees which had been cut down. What once had been a veritable Eden for loggers is now part of the Adirondack Forest Preserve, a symbol of society's interest in preserving its forested land, and a place where today's vacationers and adventurers enjoy getting out among the new-growth pine and hemlock.

A Time When Lumberjacks and Rivermen Were Heroes

© R.P. Nadeau

LIFE IN A
NORTH WOODS
LUMBER CAMP

1952. THOMAS C. O'DONNELL had just returned from a trip into the last century. He'd spent 60 years stopping over around Forestport, North Lake, the South Branch of the Moose River, Blue Mountain Lake, the big mountains of Essex County and the vast Northern Forest across Upper Michigan.

He'd met a lot of people in that logging country, which was black with tall spruce. He'd met people like camp foreman Fred Johnson, and Charles Wood, the walking boss for the Rogers Paper Company, and he was at John Negger's meat market in Forestport the Saturday night when John was showing his new rifle to John Potter and Joe Badger. Negger, with the idea the gun wasn't loaded, pulled the trigger. The bullet whizzed past Potter's head, tore a hole through the roof, and headed in the general direction of White Lake. While the bullet didn't hit Potter, it came so close to his head that "The wind grabbed aholt of my hair and whirled me around like a top," he told.

He recalled the years of long ago, when he used to drive over the rough roads to McKeever to watch the spring log drive, and his trips into the North Lake country to hunt and fish.

The people he met and those adventures never faded from his memory. When he headed in to and out from North Lake, one of the places he always stopped was Reed's Mills, where he would talk with Henry Reed and his crippled brother, Addie, who hunted quite successfully by crawling about on his hands and knees, dragging his rifle behind him.

Tom observed that in those days it appeared that the double-bitted ax "was trying to horn in on the business of dropping trees and letting in the light." Bill Jackson, of Denton & Waterbury's Camps, mindful of how an ax now and then cuts off a man's foot, said he figured he would always stick to the single-bitted ax, as "it only slices you half as often."

Tom had a connection with those rip-roaring lumbering days in the Big Woods before state-enforced lumber-harvesting regulations. Lumberjacks and rivermen were the heroes of his personal romantic saga. He was also partial to the hunters and fishermen, and to the natives who felt that game laws should not prevent them from getting enough to eat in all seasons.

For those reasons, and for the sake of documenting picturesque incidents, stories and legends of humor and adventure affecting the lives of those who lived in and roamed the lumber woods, Tom believed future generations would be grateful that he took the time to tap the lore of logging history and tell of the life of those early days he knew from personal experience.

Tom O'Donnell had a talent. He liked to tell stories about history and folklore and of the regions he lived in as a child and adult. Tom was also a skillful writer who became a noted Boonville, New York, author during the early 1950s. Some folks claimed the foothills of the Adirondacks lacked enough material to fill a book, but O'Donnell proved them wrong. In fact, readers of regional history were happily surprised to know that far from being handicapped by a dearth of material, Tom uncovered a veritable embarrassment of it.

But there was one story left untold. That story was Tom's own childhood experience of growing up in a lumber camp. He enjoyed the old timers recalling memorable events about hauling large loads of logs, about driving logs in swift river water, and felling the largest trees. He had watched the jacks play cards, arm wrestle, and throw an ax, and he'd enjoyed the camp music, especially when someone in camp could play the fiddle, mouth organ, Jew's harp or some other musical instrument.

Long before he entered school, Tom had chewed his first plug of tobacco, pitched horseshoes with the lumberjacks, and heard how a couple of younger jacks would dress as girls by tying feed sacks around their waists, and dancing with partners.

Tom said, "The history of an area is in reality the folklore of the region; things like statistics are but a detail of the story of people who have made a community. That story is made up of the humors and the tragedies of the people, of their day-by-day living, the things they say and don't say, their ways of doing and saying things."

Tom felt that if a writer can catch these things, and can relate them in a spirit of compassion and "understanding, you have done a history that is ever so much more true and full of meaning than a cold formal history could ever do."

Tom's early years were spent in an isolated section, deep in the lumber woods of America's Northern Forest in Michigan. "There exists a considerable literature devoted to lumbering operations and to the lumber camp and lumberjacks," he pointed out. "Missing, however, is a story dealing with a lumberman who might settle his family in the woods as an adjunct to his camp, affording him a home during the long operating months and an uninterrupted life with his family."

His father geared up such a plan, "but, as it worked out, the family, which would live in a grand house, became an important part of camp life and camp management." How this took place he described in an incomplete manuscript that lay dormant for fifty years following his death.

Tom freely drew from his personal experiences and his knowledge of lumbering operations, all the time questioning himself: "What not to leave out and how to condense each part of the story was the problem" explaining the "experiment," he said, "The plan under which the family became an important factor in the life of the camp was Mother's, improvised on the ground, as were many of the day-by-day decisions by which the family

became related more and more, and always beneficially, to the welfare of the [logging] crews."

As I read the manuscript, I discovered that Tom's selection of material was skillfully made, and that his chosen method of informally telling his story resulted in an interesting one. By informal, I mean that statistical and similar matter were subordinated to stories about people—his teacher and how she taught, the lumberjacks and how they did things, the rugged characters in the high timber country who imparted their woods wisdom to the O'Donnell children, the children's parents and friends, and Fred, Tom's older brother. Dates and other data of formal history are used where needed, but it is always people who dominate the telling—teachers, pals, parents, peddlers, loggers and others.

"Here was something new and beneficial," he wrote. As the logging business got in full swing, Fred, the eldest of the O'Donnell children, was

> Every man had a share in the success of the O'Donnell operation. A good motto all had in mind was "We do our part."
>
> COURTESY OF CLIFFORD H. GILL FROM
> *THE MEMOIRS OF CLIFFORD H. GILL*

leading the picture. Tom describes his brother as "Puckish in spirit, full of boyish energy, lovable beyond belief, resourceful in ideas, seemingly everywhere at the same time, one who more than any other factor dominated the spirit of the camp and house. Fred, when the camp was established was ten years of age; I his worshiping shadow, was four; Marie, then our only sister, was two, and Myrtle, yet unborn, would soon be joining us."

It was important that Tom's proposed book "would make clear the essential details of camp management and camp behavior…but above this, I discovered upon getting into the story" of his brother and sisters, was the "inspiring ingredients for a book dealing with the activities of a camp owner's family situated in the midst of a camp of lumberjacks."

Probably O'Donnell, under ordinary circumstances, would fittingly have remained a mere chronicler. But as he said, "From the start, however, I was always at Fred…persistent in my search for facts (and) answers to persistent questions." He had a notion that Fred might have considered all the questions fired at him a "nuisance, yet always Fred answered my persistent questions, whimsically or seriously as his spirit at the time might dictate.

"My brother absorbed eagerly the techniques of lumbering. At the age of thirteen he had become an accomplished rider of logs and was patiently teaching me the finer points of the art. With him I was shooting squirrels and rabbits long before we left Greendale, Michigan, and we joined in watching from close range the many bears that frequented almost to the end the creek bottoms.

"Father was a successful camp manager, although at times emitting a good deal of heat on the job. Mother was adored by the jacks and by the families of squatters who soon were coming in and settling on cutover land. It was Fred, however, who fixed the spirit of the camp as one of boisterous and infectious fun and lightheartedness. Others in the story contributed of their various qualities: Pat Moran, the school teachers, and our lumberjacks, and it is a recital of these varied exhibitions of sound business instincts, of fun and good nature, and of character, that make up the book."

Tom's lumber camp life is full of meaning—in his words, "so much better than a cold, formal history could ever do." Certainly he never forgot skidding logs by horse, the ice roads and road monkeys, Pat Moran, one of Tom's favorite jacks, and scores of other people and events. So the days of busy tote roads and sawyers, bull cooks, the barn and straw boss, the swampers, his father's authority and the big logs and tall timbers filled his mind with enough information to produce a book that is filled with tales of past lumberjack life and that at the same time is correct in all of its detail.

Tom's written memories were "conceived and written as a true and simple record of his parents experiment," he said in reflection. "I feel that the narrative will have much to interest both old and young. And equally I am certain that students of American life, and particularly of American life in unusual situations, will find in the book much to reward them.

"[My] account as told is true. The only deviation from facts is the changing of a very few names for reasons that will be obvious. It is based upon simple but sure sources. First are memories, which have not dimmed with the years. Then is correspondence over the years with principals in our Greendale life, correspondence and conversations with my sisters, and with Fred. Visits to the scene were made by the four of us at intervals of three and four years until the first World War, and since then more rarely."

And how Tom and his siblings carried on in camp! Surely, no other story he wrote provides the reader with as exhilarating an experience as this one that revives long-ago memories, always with a touch of humor. It can be safely said that Tom's clear, vivid recollections about logging camp life and living with loggers help create an accurate and interesting picture of logging as it was in the early "good old days."

Thomas C. O'Donnell's

Life in
a North Woods
Lumber Camp

Chapter One

The Family

WE LANDED, the five of us, in the township of Greendale, Midland County, Michigan, in the early hours of a March evening in 1885. We had driven in from Mount Pleasant, some ten miles to the north and west in Isabella County.

Six or eight months previously we had reached Mount Pleasant from the scenes of former timber operations carried on by Father on the Pine River in Montcalm County. There his efforts had exhausted the area's supply of timber, but he had stayed on to organize a village which, using Mother's middle name, he had called Vestaburg.

Along the Pine, at times of the spring drive, Father had performed feats of logmanship that were to become legendary. Long years later old-timers in St. Louis, halfway between Vestaburg and Saginaw, would grow eloquent as they pointed out to me the dam, down toward the end of Main Street, over which at high water in spring Father had been accustomed to ride logs, tossed this way and that by the spring flood, to the plaudits of villagers gathered for the show along the street.

© R.P. Nadeau

LIFE IN A
NORTH WOODS
LUMBER CAMP

I well knew of Father's quick, hot temper. He had been handy with his dukes, the old timers would tell me, so that when others identified him with the legendary Paul Bunyan I was not surprised. Born in Vermont of a second-generation Irish father, of Londonderry stock, he kept alive the memory of a French mother whom we children were never to know. Upstream along the Pine he had met and married my mother, who in the sweetness of her spirit was his complete opposite.

Mother was of a long line of Burgesses who, leaving Massachusetts, found themselves after a few generations in Michigan, ten years before the outbreak of the War Between the States. She was teaching school when she met and married Father.

It was not an easy life to which she gave herself in marriage. The family of a lumber baron could live in comfort and ease in a scene far removed from the husband's operations. Father was not a lumber baron, and wished to have his family near or with him. And here he was, bringing his family into the woods, where he would have day-by-day contact with his growing children. In his mind were plans for a grand house for his family, completely apart from the life of the camp to be, and when the timber was gone he would carry on as head of a many-acre farm.

Three children came with their parents that March night. Fred, the eldest, was nine years old, and I was approaching four. Marie, the baby, was learning to walk, and another, Myrtle, would arrive two years later.

From Mount Pleasant we had come in a pair of bobsleighs, reaching Greendale two or three hours after dark. I probably slept the entire distance, napping being a pastime for which I had achieved a considerable family reputation. My only memory of our arrival is of turning somersaults with Fred on stacks of bedding brought in from the sleighs and put on the floor until food had been prepared and eaten and bedtime had arrived.

We occupied, that first night and other nights until summer, a single-room log structure that had been run up to be a men's shanty, the first unit of the future camp. It was a long, low affair, two logs higher in front than at the back, so providing slope to the tarpaper-covered roof. Tarpaper was standard roofing in lumbering regions, and would be ample protection

against snow, rain and winds. Shingles, strangely, were never used for roofing in regions that were sending them in trainload lots to the world outside.

A supper was eaten with sharp appetites and, beds having been made up, the three children, warm and cozy in their flannel night things and tucked carefully in, were soon fast asleep.

My next memory is of morning and looking out through a four-pane window upon a tiny white world walled in by tall, straight pines that came up almost to the door. Nearby was a small log structure that Father had built as a temporary stable. At its door was the sleigh, its long box filled with snow that had fallen during the night.

Sometime during the morning, Mother having bundled me up, Fred took me outdoors and into the snow, which came to my chin. Memory is sketchy of the frolic that followed, but I do know that before Fred and I had really started to make the welkin ring, an unearthly quiet had pervaded the scene. Really it was no quiet at all: soft puffs of snow were dropping from trees and into the deep snow beneath; we heard the welcoming note of a chickadee, and the sweet, low note of wind moving among the tops of the trees.

Mother, whose feeling for place and location was acute, not only would be aware of all this but, I am certain, obtained from Father as they looked out of the window that morning, something of the geography of the immediate vicinity.

The narrow tote road over which he had come last night, and which passed twenty rods or so in front of the shanty, would, from the south, hail from St. Louis, joined by a road four miles out by a road from Shepherd, which lay eight miles to the southeast from our shanty.

> "Hired girls!" Father must have hit the ceiling. "Hired girls!" Revolutionary, that's what it was!

Less than a quarter of a mile to the north, Father would point out, the road over which we had come turned east, to wind an eighteen-mile way to the city of Midland. Strung upon the road would be, a few miles away, another camp and a small settlement of two.

Directly to the east, Mother would be told of the Big Salt River, a quarter of a mile away, it and its course now completely screened from view by the forest that came up to our shanty door.

"And see this little creek down here?" Father must have said, pointing toward the bottom of a sharp rise of ground. "That is Black Creek. It flows across the road just there, and empties into the Big Salt, where the river turns east to be followed by the road."

Mother would express her delight at having streams nearby, especially at having one so close as the Black Creek, which Fred used to say you could spit into from our back stoop.

"But that isn't all of the creeks," Father would say. "Here to the south a quarter mile is Potter Creek. We crossed it last night. And less than a quarter of a mile above the road Onion Creek flows across our back forty into the Potter."

Mother would then be concerned about the course of the Big Salt, and the answer would be that it followed the road, or the road followed the river, some twelve miles to the northeast, where it flowed into the Chippewa. "You may remember, Alice, that the Chippewa flows through Mount Pleasant."

At the city of Midland, Father would go on to say, the Chippewa flowed into the "Tittebawass." Father would be using the regional pronunciation of Tittabawassee, the real name of the stream, and would go on to say that from Midland the Tittebawass flowed south to Saginaw, where it joined the Pine in forming the Saginaw River.

Then Father would make clear that to the north was only timber that came down to the opposite bank of Black Creek. "And getting all that timber onto rollways and in spring on its way to Saginaw will be the work of the men in our camp."

During the day, and the days that followed, Father and Mother would be discussing plans for camp buildings that must be completed before men came into camp in the fall. There would be another men's shanty and a stable for at least nine horses. "And most of all a grand house for the family to live in, which reminds me that I forgot to mention the eating shanty for the men."

At this point, as Mother long afterward explained to me, Father received a considerable jolt.

"Why not plan our house, the big one that the family will live in—plan it big enough for the men to eat in. And of course use our kitchen too. It would be better for the hired girls—"

"Hired girls!" Father must have hit the ceiling. "Hired girls!" Revolutionary, that's what it was! Impossible.

Mother explained that the idea had just this minute come to her. "We can think about it before deciding. It might be a very good plan."

Father and Mother not only thought over the idea, but discussed it. And in the long run Father gave in. Mother would find the girls, to include a cook, and Father would include rooms for them in the house that would be, as the result of the innovation, a kind of social center for a winter's lumbering season.

Chapter Two

Spring Around the Corner

© R.P. Nadeau

LIFE IN A
NORTH WOODS
LUMBER CAMP

WE HAD BEEN in camp but two or three weeks when Father came in one evening and said we were in for a break-up. To me "break-up" was something new. It seemed to suggest danger, although there was in my mind a feeling that maybe spring was on its way.

Mother asked Father how he knew, and it was a note in her voice, I suspect, that led him to say that his remark had nothing to do with his joints. "It is just in the air, Alice. I mean spring is at our door."

We were inside the shanty at the time, but Father sniffed audibly to emphasize the point.

Others also sensed that things were stirring, for next day a half dozen men came through on their way to various lumber camps far to the north for the purpose of taking part in the spring drive. Next spring men in high, calked boots would be coming in to help in our own drive.

They came afoot, these men, each with a satchel attached to the end of a pole [known then as a "turkey"] slung over his shoulder, and each with his own and peculiar kind of headgear. There were caps of coonskin and bearskin, caps of wool, and old hats of weather-stained felt. Mackinaws were of various colors and patterns, and pants—well, just pants which, below the knee, disappeared in the tops of high, laced leather shoes, thick-soled to hold the heavy, sharp calks (pronounced "corks" in lumber woods parlance) driven into the sole and heel.

Some of the men carried their own, time-tested peaveys; others depended upon the supply they would find at their respective camps. Along the rutty road they came, with an easy, swinging gait, looking neither to right nor left, eyes on the ground in front of their feet. All were in evident hurry.

I was to learn that the migrating birds had no surer sense of impending and sudden changes in season than the lumberjack. He sensed the precise time for showing up at camp in the fall; he was keenly aware of the approach of thaws, and in spring became concerned that all skidways be emptied and logs got to the rollway at the river before a sudden thaw took from the roads the snow so vastly important during these closing hours of the winter's effort.

Some of the men stopped at our shanty for a drink of water; one or two who chanced by around the noon hour accepted Father's invitation to eat dinner with us. Almost the last caller that first day had expressed his second and third thanks and was disappearing down the road when a tall, rangy figure turned in. Father spied him instantly and called out:

"Pete Murray, you old—"

He let it go at that as Pete came up grinning.

"George O'Donnell, you old—you're a sight for these old eyes. What in—what are you doing up here, you old—"

Pete, aware of the sudden appearance of Mother and two young boys, was having difficulty with his vocabulary. Since nothing could stop him, so startling was his discovery of Father here in the woods, five minutes had passed before he reached a pause, having shaken hands with Mother and the two lads, smiling his complete happiness. It seems that Pete had worked for Father over on the Pine, but for the past two seasons had been going into the woods only for the spring drives.

An hour passed and greetings were suitably over before it occurred

Log jams in icy cold water required "whitewater men" of above average courage, determination and skill.

to Mother to ask about food. No, he hadn't eaten, and yes, he was hankering to. A lunch was soon before him, the business of eating, however, proceeding slowly by reason of Pete's accompaniment of news of dozens of lumberjacks, mutual acquaintances, up and down the Pine.

When Pete had drunk his last saucerful of tea, it was well on in the afternoon, and of course he must stay all night. "That is"—and Father indicated the nature of our restricted accommodations in a one room house—"that is if you can fix yourself up in the barn. On a pile of hay and with a lot of blankets."

"You know me, George! Anything for a chance to talk over old times."

Talk was lusty that night. Mostly it was about battles the two men had fought back in the Pine River Country. After the history of each encounter, Pete was sure to end up with, "Things ain't what they was in the old days, George, nosiree!"

Until bedtime the two men were never apart, and never silent. Father would go to the stable to bed down the horses and Pete was at his side asking if he remembered the fight that he, Pete, had that time with Red Mullen in Cedar Lake, in the Exchange Hotel bar room, an' le's see, that were in 'seventy-one, weren't it, George? Father went outside to split kindling for the fire next morning, and Pete was at his side, and all without a break in the chatter.

After supper Mother asked Pete if he remembered that song he used to sing. The one about Murphy's Camp. She would like Tommy to hear it. Pete needn't put himself out for me. Nature had neglected to wire me for sound, although Mother's repertory contained two or three little airs, used by her as croons, that I never tired of hearing. One of them, the way she sang it, I still regard as being up there with the Brahms or anybody else's lullaby:

Seven long years since Pompey was dead,
Yes, yes, Pompey was dead;
The apple tree grew right over his head,
Yes, yes, over his head.

The apples got ripe and began to fall,
Yes, yes, began to fall;
There came an old woman to gather them all,
Yes, yes, gather them all.

And so on thorough any number of stanzas to the last, which ended, I thought, on a sad and tender note:

The saddle and bridle are under the shelf,
Yes, yes, under the shelf;
If you want any more you can sing it yourself,
Yes, yes, sing it yourself.

Other than these croons of Mother's, singing left me, at the extreme age of three and growing on four, extremely cool, as did Fred's suggestion to Pete that he show us what he could do. Pete required no coaxing. He said modestly that he had been floored by a cold during the winter but would see what he could do. So it was that, encouraged by Mother, he shifted the cud of chew to the other cheek, cleared his throat, rolled his eyes to the ceiling and gave his song the works.

The chantey was typical of all camp songs, and like them was never sung twice alike. Variable too might be the name of the hero and the locale of the drama celebrated by a song; Paddy McBride might be crushed in a log jam on the Pine, and in another version it could be Bill Horkins who suffered the same tragic fate up on the Muskegon.

Mother had asked for "Murphy's Camp" and "Murphy's Camp" it was, rendered in a monotone except at the beginning and ending of each line. It had an endless number of stanzas, but as Pete sang it, eyes popping and looking straight ahead, his Adam's apple moving up and down, the performance held his audience spellbound to the end. The first stanza, which opened with "Come boys," I received with special enthusiasm, certain that it was addressed to Fred and me in a very personal kind of way:

> Come boys, if you will hear me
> I'll sing for you a song,
> And tell about the pinewoods,
> And how you get along.
> We are a jolly lot of boys,
> So merry and so fine,
> Who spend the happy winters
> A-cutting of the pine.

The song went on to describe, with commendable detail, the day-by-day life at Murphy's, and must have had a tremendous propaganda appeal in any unregenerate region in which the joys of camp life went unappreciated. In concluding it, Pete dropped the final word, with a sliding trombone effect, a full half octave, thereby informing the audience that the ballad was concluded.

Mother then asked Father to do the "Alphabet Song." The existence of such a song was news to me, a fact quite understandable since I was equally unaware of the alphabet and its considerable importance. When next winter our camp was in operation I was to hear it often enough, with a score of other songs. It was a ditty that, for best effect, had to be sung by a shantyful of men, although it was an old standby of Father's when occasion called for a solo:

A is for axes that through the woods ring,
B is for boys that can handle them so,
C is for chopping, which we all do,
And D is for danger we daily go through.

Mother, with a quick glance at me, asked Father at this point whether he ought to sing the chorus, but since that would throw him off balance, and I wouldn't understand it anyhow, what the heck, Alice, of course it's all right for him to hear it:

So merry, so merry, so merry are we,
We are the boys when we're out on a spree:
Hi-derry, ho-derry, hi-derry-down,
Give shanty boys whiskey and nothing goes wrong.

And so the song continued to play havoc with the alphabet, with letters, each four requiring a stanza of four lines and a chorus. To render the ballad called for a rugged constitution and Father's ability to complete the ordeal without a breakdown was guarantee of his health and stamina. The classy number brought the evening to a natural end, leaving Fred and me determined when we grew up to be the kind of lumberjack that Pete exemplified in deed and song.

Next morning our hero left us, but was to come back another year as a member of Father's crew, with happy and sometimes disastrous results.

Chapter Three

Heck and High Water

© R.P. Nadeau

LIFE IN A NORTH WOODS LUMBER CAMP

PETE WASN'T AWAY any too soon. The break-up two days later came in on the wings of a soft rain. Almost overnight the heavy coverlet of snow was gone and the ice, slipping its moorings, was moving down the river in huge cakes. In another twenty-four hours the Big Salt and the creeks were over their banks. What was more, the bridge over the Black Creek at the foot of our hill had disappeared.

This was a disaster of no cosmic importance, the bridge being a simple affair contrived by laying down three sleepers to reach across the creek, and upon these hewn timbers placed for flooring.

The Potter Creek Bridge was another matter. Until recently there had been no bridge over the stream. A hundred yards downstream was a ford, an affair that required the utmost in hardihood and courage of the traveler arriving from the south. It was a simple matter, when one came from St. Louis or Shepherd, or intervening points, to drop easily to the bed of the creek: To cross the creek and be confronted with an almost perpendicular wall of clay some ten feet in height was another matter. It was done, strangely enough, but its reputation, an evil one, led people who meditated a journey to points east in Greendale to postpone their trip.

I myself participated in but one heavy fording operation, and that was a year or two later, and at the Chippewa Dam, with Father at the controls. He and I were returning from Midland, Father driving Powder Face, a tall, lithe, cream-colored stallion whose fleetness of foot had become a tradition in the Pine River Country and was establishing a new one in Greendale and its environs.

We rode, Father and I, in a light, one-seated buggy, proud by reason of a dozen apple trees lying under the seat and projecting behind over the back of the box. Two Appleseed Johnnies, Greendale version! The trees would be set out south of the house and when grown—

In the midst of our dreaming, we reached the Halfway Dam Bridge, which had been taken out by high water following a two-day rain. The answer to our problem was fording the river. In days before the bridge was built, the Chippewa here was always forded—but never during high water, so far as records indicated, Father told me.

Father eased Powder Face down to the spot where in another day forders had entered, though never, I was sure, in high water. Water today, our stallion seemed to feel, was the same as water yesterday, so let's go!

To the disappointment of Powder Face, he had barely got the feel of the water than he was over his depth and was swimming for it—swimming as efficiently as ever he ran. Above the water only his head and rump could be seen. The buggy seat was an island upon which two distraught voyagers were marooned, holding on for dear life. I was scared, and since "Now I Lay Me Down to Sleep" was the only prayer I knew, I told God about our predicament, getting over the general idea that here was a swell opportunity to help a little guy and his dad out of a jam. Father, when I told him about it on the way home, seemed hurt, both for himself and Powder Face.

Ages later we reached the other side of the stream. Father, when he had disentangled his legs, got out of the buggy and went forward to make over

Powder Face. Water was dripping from the heroic cream and forming little puddles, and the stallion was shaking from the ordeal. Father stroked his face and neck and talked to him tenderly, undoubtedly trying to calm him, while Powder Face must have thought that if it was all right with us he would settle for an extra pan of oats when, if ever, he got us home.

When all this was done, Father turned to take stock of our general situation. His eye quickly took in the fact that our apple trees were gone, by this time halfway to Midland. He had failed to fasten our future cider supply to an appropriate feature of the vehicle, and there followed a session of cussing, fancy and plain, that for sheer eloquence reached a new high even for him.

During the summer, Father threw a new bridge across Potter Creek, this, like the Black Creek contrivance, a three-sleeper affair bearing a heavy plank flooring. It was lifted from its moorings next spring and its various parts distributed over two or three hundred acres of river bottoms, but a new bridge was soon laid, and when this a year later was destroyed, Father ordered an iron affair which he had placed upon foundations rising high above high water mark, and on the low ground of the bottoms, hauling in sand to prevent any future trouble. The bridge was still in use the last time I saw Greendale.

Water, far more than the immediate details of running a camp, supplied the lumberman's anxieties. Whether there was sufficient water in the streams next spring determined how much if any of his harvest of logs would reach market at Saginaw, and a log left on a rollway, or stranded high and dry along a river, was worth nothing.

Too much water, on the other hand, might hold its minor disasters. Logs floating downstream on a river well over its banks had a way of bolting the normal course, spreading themselves over the flats in the absence of enough river men on the job to keep the timber properly shepherded within the banks.

Just how much water there would be in the spring would be determined by the amount of snow that had fallen during the winter. Snow thus served the double purpose of making it possible to sled the logs to

the rollways from the cutting areas, and then in spring furnishing the water necessary to get the harvest to market.

Ruin overtook more than one lumberman who attempted to operate on a capital too small to carry him past a snowless winter or two. These would be, not the big operators, men who were able to manage their camps by remote control, with ample backlogs of credit, but the small men. Some of these kept barely a jump or two ahead of the sheriff anyhow, and were always at the mercy of some caprice of the weather. Theirs were the heartaches and the headaches. Being hard-bitten men of the woods, theirs also were the thrills that came of close contact with their kind of men, sharing their dangers, and their simple lives of robust pleasures.

Father was such an operator, and now that spring was at the door, it was high time to think about work upon the camp that was to be. He had engaged the necessary men, carpenters and others, to come in and put up our buildings. Plans and other details were soon completed, and one June morning the sound of falling timber began to be heard right in our backyard. Trees were being felled and sawn into logs of necessary lengths for the home of the family, the first building to be completed. Logs were hewn by men swinging broad axes, but not before two men, one at either end of a log, held along the log a stout cord over which a blob of blue chalk had been run and which when raised and allowed to snap against a log left a blue line to which the men with broad axes would hew.

Etched deeply in our memory too was the thin cry of planes as they cut along the edges of boards for flooring, and the sweet, pitchy smell of the coils of pine shavings.

All this activity thrilled Fred and me. Etched deeply in our memory too was the thin cry of planes as they cut along the edges of boards for flooring, and the sweet, pitchy smell of the coils of pine shavings.

The climaxing excitement for the younger fry, however, came with the discovery that the limbs and tops of the fallen trees were to be stacked in piles and burned. This would mean roaring fires that would shoot flames to near the tops of trees. Such fires would be thrilling enough in daytime, when the fires were set, but they would continue to roar and snap and crackle well on into the night, the sky becoming a sinister, glowing sea of flame, and the men tending the fires and the surrounding trees would be dark shadows edged with red.

At last the house was completed, the family moved in, and work was begun on other buildings. These were scattered in an area some fifty yards back from the house. They were arranged in a rough approximation to a plan, having as their center of interest the stable. At right angles to this stood, when completed, a wagon house. In a general line with this and facing the barn were a granary, a tool house, and lastly, with little relation to the main group of buildings, was the shanty in which we had been living. A second shanty for men stood across the road from the house, and across Black Creek was built a blacksmith shop.

The other buildings were not grand like our house. Their logs were not hewn, and they did not have French windows and fancy doors with panels containing red, yellow and green glass panes. In front, between the house and the road, was a wall of fieldstone two feet high, and in the center three stone steps to assist you down the considerable slope from the house to the highway in front.

The stable and other related buildings, I afterwards learned, would in time be torn down and to take their place a handsome frame structure would be erected, along with other essential buildings. This would be when, our timber gone, Father would embark upon the career of gentleman farmer.

To my untutored taste, the stable deserved to stand forever, so majestic were its dimensions and its general aspect. For a log building it was huge and pretentious. In design it followed the form of barns common to farming regions, even to a gambrel roof. This kind of roof was news to me. To my ear it had a sound strangely reminiscent of what men in the shanty played with chips nights after the axes were ground, saws filed and set, and shirts, undershirts and drawers overhauled for delousing and repairs. In the center of the front elevation were wide, swinging doors opening to the floor of the barn; to the left as one entered was the row of stalls for the horses, with space above the ceiling for the mowing away of hay. At the other end of the barn was a similar arrangement of stalls, with stanchions for cows, and above, a ceiling, more room for hay.

By the end of August, the camp was finished and a month later lumberjacks engaged by Father began to arrive. They came, some thirty of them, from all directions—from the regions of the Pine to the south, from Clare and Gladwin to the northeast, and from Saginaw and Bay City. Each arrived with a turkey slung over his shoulder, stuffed with a wide assortment of objects, from a pair of Sunday pants to a deck of playing cards and a few plugs of Jolly Tar or other chewing tobacco, handkerchiefs, razor, knife and other items for which there would be room. The contents might vary in the matter of some items, but one object was a must in any jack's turkey: a red bandana handkerchief, to be wound around the neck for Sunday adornment, especially useful should chance at any time bring into their proximity a member of the fairer sex.

Chapter Four

Poker
à la Jerry

© R.P. Nadeau

LIFE IN A
NORTH WOODS
LUMBER CAMP

FOR MY MONEY, the most glamorous of the new crew was the chore boy, Jerry Kerr. Jerry variously reported himself as seventeen, eighteen, and up to twenty years of age. His genius had been picked up, not as might be supposed, for some unusual talent, but rather, as one day I heard Father explain to Mother, because he was too dumb even to want to be a scaler.

On Father's list of favorite aversions, scalers easily held top rating. The fact lent no particular distinction to the profession, Father having so many aversions that to this day I cannot conceive by what method he kept them tagged in his mind. In the list, to name but a few, were Republicans, white horses, boiled onions, bathing suits, the entire Gannon family (although he employed three of them, including the father) and, as befitted an Irishman, the Prince of Wales.

The scaler aversion seemed grounded in the belief, first that scalers were too dumb to count up to ten (which was bad since mathematics figured so prominently in the profession), and second, that the entire lot of them had cysts in their eyes. This latter conviction was based possibly on an encounter with some otherwise harmless specimen of the breed, whose slightest eye trouble would be exalted by Father into the character of a cyst. Whether he had a clear notion of the nature of a cyst, or of where cysts were to be found, I would never know. It would have been like him in any case to go for such a word in a big way and, intrigued by its sinister sound, use it as a symbol for all and sundry kinds of cussedness.

The scaler was never employed by the lumberman, but by the Boom Company in Saginaw, buyer of our logs. In the large camps, the scaler came in with the men in the autumn and was kept busy until the break-up in the spring. For the smaller camps, however, he came in at the fag end of the season and would be able to clean up the job in a few days. Even this, according to Father, was too long.

A scaler assigned to a large camp would remain throughout the day on a rollway and, with a long logging rule, find the diameter of each log as it was hauled in and rolled off the sleigh. Consulting rows of figures on the sides of the rule, he determined the number of cubic feet contained in a log of that diameter and a given length. The figure he put in a book, and the book at the end of a season would yield the winter's crop in terms of total footage.

Immediately behind the scaler came a man wielding a sledge-like iron bearing in raised figures the lumberman's mark. Father's mark, was, as our lingo always explained, "4 bar D." Each end of a log was given several impressions of the mark. For ears attuned to music, the marking of logs produced sounds that would challenge the capacity of any organ or orchestra. The notes given off by large logs, by small logs, and logs of various sizes in between, especially if reaching the ear from a distance of a quarter or half mile, could never be reproduced by any instrument devised by man.

The very nature of a scaler's work made it a simple matter for Father to consider the gentry as a set of rascals, scalawags and cheats, bent only on serving their masters and cheating the lumberman. Whatever was the cause of his attitude, it could easily have been that the scaler sent into his first camp was a firm believer in infant damnation.

TOPPING OUT SKIDWAY.
No 6.

Log sleighs were built solid with three-and-a-half-foot length runners, three-and-a-half-foot wide beams and four-foot bunks connected together by a short neap.

Low as were Father's estimates of Jerry's intellectual capacities, to me he was Mister Allure himself. He gave me a new outlook on life and the world. Hitherto the latter had been a place where you ate and slept, and followed the very worthy and engaging pastime of being always at Fred's heels, an adoring shadow. Now, however, under Jerry's tutelage, I began to extend my interests into new and unsuspected fields.

Each morning Jerry was up and about hours before the cracking of dawn and, while the men emerged from their bunks, climbed into their garments, performed sketchy ablutions and ate their breakfast, Jerry was feeding, currying and harnessing the horses. After seeing the last team off for the woods and eating his own breakfast, he retired to the shanties to straighten bunks, sweep floors, and perform such little tasks as would ready the places for the men when they came in at night. Similarly, the stables would have to be readied, but after a morning's session with me in the mysteries of poker, there would be plenty of time for such paltry duties.

First after his arrival came Jerry's introduction of me into the intricacies of poker. Great was his dismay when he found that I could not perform the simple feat of counting all my fingers. This defect he set out to correct, devoting our first session entirely to that worthy purpose.

"What is that?" he asked, holding up his index digit.

"Your finger," I replied, which I felt to be pretty good for so young a kid.

"I know it's a finger, but how many?"

I sensed a new note in Jerry's voice, but I replied promptly, "How many what?"

"How many fingers!"

"Why?"

The dialogue was becoming involved for both of us, but for me it can be said that my poise was better than Jerry's, who next held up the ace of spades.

"What is that?"

"Ace of spades," I replied smartly.

Jerry was trying to believe his ears. "Oh my gosh! Where did you get that?" With these questions I returned to normal and replied:

"I ain't got it. You got it."

At that particular stage of my education in games of chance, all playing cards were aces of spades, so that when Jerry held up the three of hearts for identification, I came up with the ringing statement, "Ace of spades!"

Jerry all but fell off the bench on which we sat astride, facing each other. "I give up," he moaned, a statement which I countered with a stinging, "Give up what?"

This, so far as I was concerned, could have gone on for hours, but Jerry picked up the cards and the handful of beans that he had dedicated to service as chips, and dashed for asylum to the stable. Here he began setting the stalls to rights and filling the mangers with hay and the feed boxes with oats.

Jerry was not a quitter. I was no simple case for his ministrations, wherefore he assumed full responsibility for my training in mathematics (poker could come later) and devoted an hour or more daily to that worthy purpose.

The campaign went on until Christmas, by which time my advancement enabled me to identify a jack of clubs or a trey of diamonds with the best of them. For a time I was stalled in the higher realms of the subject, full houses and bobtail flushes giving me no end of trouble, though in the long run Jerry made even these for me an open book.

For some reason unknown to me, Jerry seized this point in my tutelage to turn to checkers, but before I was able ever to get a man in the king row the spring break-up was upon us and Jerry was away on the drive, resplendent, as he left us that last morning, in heavy calked boots that encased the calves of his legs, and a peavey over a shoulder.

IN A BURST of candor that elevated him a notch or two in Father's estimation, Jerry had announced at the end of the drive that he would not return to camp in the fall. No amount of quizzing revealed where he would be and why he was leaving. The truth like as not was that his future was a dark mystery, and that he was fed up with being constantly hazed by the men.

In spite of his love of strutting before the likes of me, Jerry was the perfect fall guy for camp humorists. Against them he had little or no defense. I recall but once his getting his evenings, that being the time that Joe Wagner, a sawyer from down around Pontiac, taught him a song filled with double entendres, words and air so simple that even Jerry could master the piece without prolonged effort. So tender a lyric, he was told, must be sung to Nellie Keogh, one of the hired girls.

Next morning, when he had finished his last cup of coffee, with Nellie cleaning things from the table, Jerry went into the routine, only to have a platter crack down on his head and barely missing a butcher knife tossed at him with dexterity and spirit.

Chapter Five

Pat Moran Limps in

© R.P. Nadeau

LIFE IN A
NORTH WOODS
LUMBER CAMP

Lumberjacks were hearty eaters. California prune cake was a favorite cook room recipe served on tin plates.

COURTESY OF GEORGE SHAUGHNESSY

Nellie's tactics gave Jerry an idea for getting back at Joe. Surprise! Let Joe have it when and where he least expected it. During the day he watched for a moment when he could lift Father's shotgun, an old muzzleloader, from its place under our stairway. Loading it with an extra finger of powder, but without lead, Jerry that night, when all were asleep, stole from his bunk, slid quietly to the floor alongside Joe's, and fired.

Before the camp could recover from its collective surprise, Jerry was back in bed and doors up at the house were slamming, a sign that Father was up and about. A moment or two later, he dashed into the shanty, a mackinaw over his nightshirt, only to find every man asleep!

Next autumn Old Pat Moran was installed in Jerry's place. As an intellectual stimulus, he was a positive advance over his predecessor. A white-haired veteran of the War Between the States, it seems that at Cold Spring a minié ball caught Pat in the right instep. In due time, he was returned to his native Boston. He carried a souvenir of the battle with him ever after—a considerable limp, requiring a cane for effective navigation. For all his years and his handicap, he was spry and energetic, dashing about with a weaving motion that simulated a column of infantry in motion.

Pat's interests were vastly nobler, and broader in their scope, than Jerry's had been, and his methods of instruction were more successful. And he was a devoted and an artful fisherman.

From the first, Old Pat was bent upon instilling in my mind a comprehensive view of the war, within the compass of those battles that, practically single-handedly, he had won for a none-too-grateful country. Happily, his pedagogies were such as would not be diluted by giving a lecture on battle techniques. With eyes glued fixedly on a bobber, he could be equally intent as he described scenes in any of the battles fought along the Pamunkey River.

"Yes sir, as I was a-telling ye, Tom," he might be saying, "me company had been fighting like the old devil himself. Six times the Rebs in front of us charges and six times we throws them back. But our lines were getting thin, Tom. Yes sir, too dom thin. We was ordered to fall back but the company was cut off, and all t'onct a shell comes along and gets the Captain, and as he lays there bleeding he sends for me and says, says he, Pat, says he, 'I'm done for,' says he. 'Take the company, Pat,' says he, 'what is left of it,' says he, 'and give them hell,' and he dies right there that very minute, Tom. So I grabs up his sword and yells. 'Follow me, me men!' says I, and they lets out a yell and …"

Pat's cork would suddenly start bobbing violently and then go under a good foot. The old soldier, who had worked himself into a state of the greatest excitement in his war recollections, would give a yank at the pole, bringing the line flying back through the air and catching high in a blue beech just back of us. Heroic exploits the theme of the hour, I handed my fishing pole to Pat and presently had shinnied up the smooth trunk of the tree and was releasing the hook. Presently our bobbers were floating again, and we had taken up details of the charge leading up to the denouement. It seems that the enemy fell back in a rout so complete that the Colonel sent for Pat to bestow upon him the accolade of his praise.

"And there was the Colonel, Tom, as big as life. And he come up to me and says, says he, 'Pat,' says he, 'you're the domdest, fightingest man,' says he, 'in the whole dom army,' says he. 'Me hond, Pat!' says he."

Pat, no doubt about it, was a specialist in heroic charges. When things were at their worst on any field of battle, always the commanding officer (most commonly the commander of a brigade, and not infrequently of a corps) would, if he had any sense at all, shove Pat in there and tell him to do his domdest. And, the flag planted in some captured work, the C.O. would tell Pat that he was the bravest dom man in the whole dommed army and give him his hond.

Under Pat's tuition, I gained a decided bias in favor of the kind of battle in which troops are always charging back and forth, particularly if, leading the charge, was a flaming spirit like Pat, firing his men to exploits of the greatest daring and courage. Battles in which you just lob shells from your big guns over into enemy territory and the enemy lobs them back left me completely cold.

No less did Pat leave his influence upon my fishing techniques. He belonged to the school that held it a waste of time and energy to go traipsing up and down a stream trying to lure your prey with phony insects and such. Just sit down on the bank, your feet hanging to within an inch of the water, ram a fresh piece of Jolly Tar into your cheek, drop a fat worm into the pool, and from that point on leave the whole business to the fish.

Sleeping arrangements for Pat shifted with the seasons. Summers, when the men's shanties were vacant, he appropriated a bunk that by preemption belonged to Emory Lewis, who hailed from over Bay City way and was the first man to report at camp our first year. Winters, partly because Pat, as Jerry had been, was the object of no little camp humor, and partly because he was expert at building morning fires, just as long before he had been wont to fire soldiers to epic exploits, Pat was given a small bedroom in the house, just off the kitchen, within quick range of the cook stove.

Starting a morning fire always, with Pat, began the previous afternoon, when the old soldier went to the woodshed back of the house and split a block of dry pine into sticks around an inch square. These he would bring into the house, an armful of them, and that night, when he had bedded down the horses and generally made things nice and cozy, he would sit by the kitchen stove and whittle shavings against the morning fire. His knife always at razor edge, the technique was to seize a stick at one end and carve a long, thick curling shaving, which at the very bottom of the stick he left attached. This performance he would repeat around and around the stick, until finally the completed project resembled nothing so much as a grand shower of glorious shavings ready for entry in a contest at some whittling show.

The entire armful of sticks thus disposed of, Pat would enter his room, close the door modestly behind him, and go to bed. The rest of the night he would have rewarding dreams of the time when at Cold Spring some appreciative General had Pat brought to his tent and gave him his hond.

Chapter Six

Angling Made Difficult

© R.P. Nadeau

LIFE IN A NORTH WOODS LUMBER CAMP

THE END of our first lumbering season had come with the spring drive. The water was at last back within the banks of the streams. Leeks and wild onions along Potter Creek, acres of them, reared wan heads above the film of silt left by the high water and cast a perfume of sorts on the air. Skies were blue and filled with the chattering of squirrels and the riveter effects of the pecking of woodpeckers.

The family at last were alone, Father and Mother with their thoughts and plans for next winter, and the children inducting themselves into a summer of fun for which the lengthening days were always too short. Marie in July would relinquish her position of last on the roster of children in favor of a very new recruit to our rounds of fun, Myrtle, a new baby.

The new infant, Fred confided to me, would more or less be dumped into our laps. He probably had the same misgivings about me upon my arrival, though I had easily solved that problem by doing the dumping myself, into his lap. How well he bore up under the burden had been written, I hope, in letters of gold in the records of that bright land where years ago he took his place, blithest of all, I am certain, in that throng of gay young spirits who, in the wisdom of the Great Boss, seem always to be called early, for the express purpose no doubt of keeping heaven young.

Meditating upon our experience with Marie, Fred could have no reason to fear that our style would be cramped. Both of us had dumped her in Mother's lap. I cannot remember that either of us ever paid the slightest attention to her, and she fully reciprocated the attitude. Playthings were always cluttering the house, and it was Father and Mother, not Fred and I, who were obliged to sing to her, interminably at some sessions.

Marie soon adopted Myrtle as her own very personal charge, and did it with an enthusiasm that Fred and I heartily applauded. For me, suckers were already abroad in the streams, and they would be followed by rock bass, and these in turn by shiners and horned dace. To cope with them demanded my undistracted attention. Fred scorned so sedentary an occupation and took over such stable activities as Pat's infirmities unfitted him for. Exercising the horses in summer was chief of his self-assumed jobs, and exercising nine horses, as Fred did through the first weeks of the summer, could easily become a career.

In Fred's layout of his activities, outstanding was his combination of work and pleasure. Instead of quenching a horse's thirst with a pail of water, he conceived of a plan by which he rode each horse to Potter Creek and back. Such a program piled up a riding total for Fred of more than fifteen miles each day. These were not everyday miles, but miles ridden bareback and without halter or bridle. He did work on a stunt that he had seen in a circus, namely, standing on an animal's back. Fred was a rein-less rider, however, for hanging onto a rein was beneath any woodsman! Altogether there were five months of this, and no doubt the animals viewed with the greatest enthusiasm the return of the lumberjacks and of settled habits in the autumn.

For myself, I had dedicated the summer to fishing. This could have been a solo venture but when Fred took over the care of the horses, Pat was released to spend his days with me on the creeks.

It must be kept in mind that except in times of high water the streams on a straight-away run would seldom reach above the knees. Let a creek make a sharp bend, however, and the current had scooped out a deep pool along the outer rim of the bend. The bottom at this point would be cluttered with dead-head logs and various other kinds of debris. Such places were made for fish—a view that for a long time I held to as a literal fact, heaping unstinted praise upon those persons who had thought it up.

These "fishing holes" might be from an eighth to a quarter mile apart. To get from one to another, with a long fishing pole, the line forever catching in the rank undergrowth, was, what with Pat's limp and cane, asking too much of the hero of Cold Spring.

Pat overcame the difficulty by having a pole for each pool. Upon leaving a hole, his routine was to take his line from the pole, wind it with extreme care on a spindle, which he had whittled from a bit of pine, and shove the pole inside a hollow log nearby. He would then hobble to the next hole, where was another log concealing a pole. An all-day fishing jaunt meant a prodigious supply of poles, but the Greendale swales were equal to Pat's demands.

In the swales grew dense thickets of black ash saplings, tall and straight like bamboo and of appropriate diameters. Let one of them reach a thickness of an inch or an inch and a quarter, and it would die, from, I surmise, a lack of room and sunlight. A swale presented a striking appearance in winter, the mass of gray blue which they offered standing out vividly against a backdrop of green pine and hemlock.

In these places were Pat's supplies of fishing poles. A sapling had scarcely died than its strength was gone, wherefore Pat was always cutting them green, a fact that would add lightness to its other qualities, and for seasoning he would stow them away in the stable.

Pat was never content with a short line. If a line came in a fifty-foot length he would wind it along the pole to near the grip end, and then back again, allowing himself sufficient length of free line to reach any part of a pool. A neat knot ended the preparations for fishing as soon as a worm had been impaled upon the hook.

It was not all work and no play
in O'Donnell's lumber camp.

COURTESY OF THE TOWN OF WEBB
HISTORICAL SOCIETY

The astonishing fact is that on leaving a hole for the next one, the line must be unwound, then wound onto a bobbin and the pole concealed inside a hollow log, and the entire procedure reversed at the next hole. The log, it may be added, seldom assured secrecy of the hideaway. More often than not, the pole would project from the end of the log, up to three or four feet of it.

The handling of bait was a matter of extremist simplicity. Pat never carried a can for worms. Angleworms, as many as could be used, were found along the river bottoms by turning over a log and similar drift left by high water. Arrived at a pool, even before fetching a pole, Pat began foraging for bait, which he put in the crown of his hat onto a layer of grass or ferns, dampened by swishing in water. The hat he then put in place on his head.

Such were Pat's fishing techniques, all of which I adopted in detail as professional, prescribed, and proper procedure. The only difference in our techniques was that when I could not find at a pool a second log, I put my pole in the log that by all good rights was his and his alone.

A pool could be cleared out in an hour or two. This didn't mean that you had extracted all the fish from it. Your state of mind could determine how long you hung around a pool. If all was jack [all right] between you and the world, you might stay at a pool most of the day, bites or no bites, just sitting on the bank, feet dangling over, and keeping the old eye eternally on the bobber—usually a cork from a ketchup bottle.

> When a fish did fall for a worm, Pat was prepared to cope with the situation... in a spirit of extreme optimism, he had cut a small branch... to thread the tip of it through the gills of a fish and on through the mouth and draw the fish down to the end... The fish would then be lowered into the water... the branch held secure by a rock...

When a fish did fall for a worm, Pat was prepared to cope with the situation. Already, in a spirit of extreme optimism, he had cut a small branch from the limber but tough blue beech, trimming it in such a way that he had only to thread the tip of it through the gills of a fish and on through the mouth and draw the fish down to the end, where it came sharp against a four or five inch section of a branch, cut at this point for the purpose. The fish would then be lowered into the water and the tip of the branch held secure by a rock placed upon it.

Each had his own carrier, and when along toward supper time we returned home, Mother would meet me and cry, "Oh, what a wonderful fish," at the same time casting an eye of wonder at the collection brought in by Pat.

Pat must sometimes have preferred to be alone, unencumbered by my presence, that he might with greater concentration meditate upon the time when some general had given him his hond. Whenever my gaze fell upon a log left by high water upon a bank, I must roll it into the stream, mount it and set out upon a one-man drive. Let it catch upon a sandbar from which I could not dislodge it with an improvised pike pole, my cue was to jump in, pants and all, and give the log a mighty shove into the current.

All this, and particularly the splash as the log hit the water, was visibly distracting to the old veteran. Always aware, however, that since there was no telling when he might need me, he kept a grip on his emotions. To get to the deep sides of pools that lay on the opposite side of a creek, any real angler must cross on some tree that had been blown down and lay across the stream. Here I was as good as indispensable unless Pat was content to spend all day on one side of the river and pass up better pools on the other side.

Many hazards confronted Pat as he negotiated a fallen tree sprawled across a stream. Limbs stuck out in all directions, and while inching one's way along, it was necessary to put the arms around the upright ones, throw a leg around to sure footing beyond, then follow gingerly with the other. One had the sensation through most of the adventure of dangling over black, fathomless water below. The ordeal was particularly perilous if the tree did not reach quite across, because the fisherman must manage the last two or three feet without benefit of any armistice except of healthy leap.

In all such operations, holding tight to Old Pat was where I had my uses. If, of course, it had come into the old man's mind to drop off a tree, I would have been powerless to prevent the tragedy. My presence probably had a prodigious moral value, and that would mean much for the man who had been the toast of generals. The perilous undertaking, of course, required a good deal of doing, but it can be reported that I never failed to get my man across.

Chapter Seven

Jut Loves Arnie

© R.P. Nadeau

LIFE IN A
NORTH WOODS
LUMBER CAMP

AMONG THE HANDS rounded up for our second camp season was Jut Gannon. The season after that, he was accompanied by his father, a widower, and a year later also by a brother. So far as I know, Jut had no sinister purpose in bringing in his family piecemeal. The business must have managed itself, unurged by any motives from outside.

Whatever the Gannons did was performed in the same purposeless and casual way. All three were huge fellows, powerful, and with red hair and hot tempers.

For all of his physical strength, Jut never could have dreamed that one day he would achieve immortality by appearing in a book made up of Michigan lumber camp songs. In the book was a dirge relating the tragic and heroic fate that befell Jut while driving logs on the Muskegon River. It seemed to me incredible; there must have been two Juts. I inquired of the author of the book and received a reply that there could not possibly have been two Jut Gannons, a conclusion that I could readily accept.

The job to which Father assigned Jut was not calculated to bring out any latent heroic qualities in any man's career. In our camp he was a rosser, and rossers, next to scalers, were at the bottom of Father's I.Q. list. Father declared that the job required no brains at all, although presenting his views with a vehemence that aroused in me a feeling that the matter deserved looking into. Hanging around Jut amply justified Father's conclusions.

A rosser was a man who, when a tree had fallen, came up with an ax to remove the bark, halfway around, from one end of each log, into which the tree would be sawn. Whether the log was drawn to a nearby skidway or snaked out, the peeled end of the log would considerably ease the labor of the horses. From the rollway to the bank of the river, logs would be piled high on sleighs that creaked under the weight of fifteen, twenty, and even more logs, a volume that

For all of his physical strength, Jut never could have dreamed that one day he would achieve immortality by appearing in a book made up of Michigan lumber camp songs.

aroused no enthusiasm in the team. Such is the superiority of practice over exegesis, of course, that by the time this point had been made, Jut would have seen logs from two or three additional trees headed towards the skidway.

Lest the word "dray" seem to indicate a vehicle more majestic than the woods dray really was, it should be made clear that the vehicle, constructed in the camp, consisted of two runners held together by a bunk halfway back from the front end, where was a "nose," with a hole through which a chain, attached to the bunk, was wrapped around the log to hold it in place. The front end of the chain was attached to the rear of the horses for hauling purposes.

Jut, like his father and brother, was a tall, heavyset, red-haired giant, given to tall talk about imaginary exploits on previous jobs, wherefore nobody was surprised when, his first morning out, he quickly showed up at the house asking Father for a left-handed handspike. He had dashed a good two miles through the woods.

"They said you would know where to find one, George!"

Father's face was a study, mostly betraying the thought, "I was right!"

Suddenly he burst into a laugh that brought Mother to the door, asking what the hilarity was about.

Father explained, and when Mother asked what was so funny about that, for reply Father went down to the stable and selected not one but three of the largest and heaviest lengths he could find from a stock of assorted pieces cut from the toughest and heaviest of all woods found along the river, the ironwood.

"Here you are," Father told Jut. "You will have to take all three—they didn't say whether they wanted a ten-degree or a twenty or thirty."

Jut's education was extended later by a woodchuck hunt one dark night far up on Onion Creek. This was Greendale's version of the ancient and reliable snipe hunt, like it in all essentials, and equally uplifting and educational.

Some of the implications of the handspike episode told me that all might not be well with Jut. I took my problem to Fred, who informed me that Jut was sweet on Arnie, one of our two hired girls that year. I asked what that was and whether it was good. Fred's answer was that I was too young to know, a reply that fully reinstated Jut in my original high opinion.

Arnie to me left a good deal to be desired. Better teamwork between her eyes, for one thing. They crossed and everything but criss-crossed each other, to the extent that when one day she asked me what I was saying, Fred told her to mind her damn business. The men bantered her as she served dinner, her plump figure, in a brown gingham dress, bobbing about with an efficiency that, in spite of restrictions in her intellectual gifts, won her the almost complete approbation of Mother.

I was always on the watch for any symptoms of Jut being sweet on Arnie, and the only thing I observed was that he was always hanging around her. He was the first one at the table, just as he was the last to leave, and once I overheard him say "Oh gosh!" in response to a giggle. Often he found an excuse to come to the house in the evening—tonight for a needle or thread, tomorrow night for a button or a patch for his overalls. Always he was hanging around, and until a year later, when I began to hang around Nora Jones, the phrase "Oh gosh!" told me that a boy was sweet on a girl.

One evening, at the end of a bitter, cold day, talk turned at supper to the weather and the skies. Fred, who was permitted to eat with the men, came up with one of his big ideas.

Timber was cut with crosscut saws and drawn to skidways.
COURTESY OF EARL M. KREUZER

"Like to look at the Big Dipper through a telescope tonight, Arnie?"

Arnie giggled a response and George Kent suggested that it be made a twosome, Jut also taking part. The hour was set for eight o'clock, when the Big Dipper, Fred made clear, would be in just the right place.

While Jut, dinner over, still clung to the dining room, Fred was in the lower shanty helping to complete plans for the excursion into astronomy, wherefore at the appointed hour Arnie and Jut where taken onto the back stoop, across which swept a bitter wind from the northwest. The sleeves of a mackinaw were held up, the two neophytes were placed cozily close to each other and told each to gaze through a sleeve at the beautiful sight. As Jut's arm was starting to steal about Arnie's waist, Fred and George at a signal emptied dippers of ice-cold water down the "telescopes," to the hilarious delight of Arnie. Jut wanted to go through it again, but Fred observed Mother coming towards the window and said they must wait for a colder night.

In his pursuit of Arnie's education, Fred's greatest achievement came that winter when he taught her how to coast down hills. Our blacksmith had made sleds for Fred and me—not too much to look at, but with runners of bent hickory, and steel shod—and long enough to let you lie full length without your feet dangling far behind.

Halfway down the slope from the house to the road, Father had built a two-foot wall of stones taken from the riverbed. This in summer afforded a pleasing terrace effect, and in winter provided a perfect site for our flirtations, as we conceived them, with death. The snow had no sooner become packed than we improvised sprinklers by driving nails through the bottoms of oyster cans and with these spread water up and down the hill until we had a wide run of glare ice. At the bottom of the hill, it was merely a matter of braking a sled with a foot to turn us into the road and on down as far as the bridge over Black Creek.

Over the course Arnie was inducted into the mysteries of bobsledding; knowledge, Fred being as he was, would of course come the hard way. The first flight got off to a complete success when Fred got Arnie poised for the run. Placing her on the sled, sitting bolt upright, he raised her arms straight above her head, cautioning her to keep them so. Then a smart shove of the sled and she was off. She reached the terrace in a time that equaled Fred's best, but she had not been instructed in the art of taking the drop at the point.

By this time I feared for the worst, and shut my eyes against Arnie's certain doom. When I opened them, it was to see her emerging from a drift of snow far to the right of the course, rubbing snow from her eyes and tittering in unfeigned delight. She asked for the run all over again, and again and again, wearing Fred down to the point where I at last heard him tell her to go to hell.

That night Arnie told Jut about it, and couldn't she show him the knack of it? She could, and, finding the sleds, they went to the launching site. Arnie told Jut how to sit, just so, and to hold his arms straight above his head. Then she added to Fred's formula by telling Jut to shut his eyes. By now the entire camp was out to see the demonstration.

Jut might have come through the ordeal without scathe except that he sailed from the sled in too sweeping an arc and, overshooting the snowdrift, collided head on with a stump that Father had been too busy to remove.

When Arnie's hero came to, it was in a bed rigged up for him in the living room of the house. Here for a week he was tended for what was diagnosed in and around the environs as a broken neck. Arnie assigned to herself the job of ministering to his comfort, and I asked Fred what it meant when a woman hangs around a man. He didn't answer.

Chapter Eight

Salesman Unlimited

© R.P. Nadeau

LIFE IN A
NORTH WOODS
LUMBER CAMP

FATHER AND MOTHER had come through their first family-owned logging company operating season with a good deal of success, and word of the fact must have reached those far-away places where tin peddlers, itinerant photographers and such would learn of the fact. In any event, all of the gentry seemed determined to beat a route to our door without delay.

The first to arrive came in July, a dispenser of notions in exchange for old rags, driving a one-horse wagon. On the conveyance was an enclosed and ample box-like space in which were bolts of calico and other fabrics, pins, needles, buttons, hats no less, and do-dads for the more fastidious of possible customers. Such items would be exchanged for old clothes and rags, which would be packed into burlap bags and attached to the wagon in spaces visible and invisible to the naked eye.

When the lumberjacks had left camp at the end of our first season, Mother had retrieved from the shanties a considerable quantity of castoff garments left by the jacks. When washed by Arnie, they seemed well-suited for the express purpose of exchanging for finery such as the visitor's wagon displayed.

A deal necessitated a good deal of haggling, Mother knowing her peddlers. Figures would be eventually arrived at, and out of the transaction Marie would acquire a new dress, Fred and me a cap apiece, with pins and needles and other notions for Mother.

Our peddler, the transaction concluded, looked at the sky and then at the sun and suggested that maybe we could put him up for the night. We could, and over the evening meal there was much talk, of sorts, about places the guest had seen, and of one or two families that Father and Mother knew out in the Pine River country. Arnie had made up a bed in one of the men's shanties, to which he repaired, in undoubted relief from questions and unrelated observations which my brother Fred and I were always introducing into the conversation for the night.

In our backwoods community any peddler with a horse-drawn wagon or carrying his "packs" was welcome. The traffickers brought news of the outside world, furnished needed goods, and provided bits of social amenities and neighborly news or some word of more widespread country or state happenings to our secluded life. Whomever the salesperson, a warm greeting was always delivered.

Whatever was delivered, peddlers—not always called by that name—played a part in shaping personalities, as surely as the thread sold by the peddler went into the shaping of a garment Mother sewed.

At breakfast next morning our merchant inquired with respect to possible customers along the road. Mother gave him enthusiastic reports about the Gibbses and their neighbors. Mrs. Gibbs, according to her report to Mother, suggested to the dispenser of notions that the scarcity of settlers between them and the city of Midland should be considered. Nothing daunted, however, the peddler continued on his way, and since, such as it was, all this was virgin territory he reached Midland with his stock of goods all but gone, but with his wagon heaped to the sky with old rags, as we learned later.

When our breakfast was concluded that morning, our guest must repay Mother for his overnight entertainment, and bestowed upon her the remains of a bolt of brown muslin.

Word in time must have reached other peddlers of notions, for next summer three similar outfits passed through, Barney (thus at his request we were to call him) and his wagon included. Each of the three did a rousing business at our establishment, Barney in particular, he being the first to pass through. Each stayed overnight, a fact that added mightily to our swag in the form of gifts which each bestowed upon Mother.

The second peddler had barely gone when a book salesman knocked at our door. He was representing "…a New York publishing company, Mrs. O'Donnell, and my purpose in calling is to bring to your attention a new book just off our presses." Without so much as a hesitation in his spiel, he lifted from a bag a huge volume which, he declared, gave a true and exciting account of the discovery and rescue of Doctor Livingston by James Gordon Bennett. "A book, Mrs. O'Donnell, that must be placed in the home of every red-blooded American!"

For this one we would have to part with some money. From the young man's description, I could see that the author had pulled all the stops out, so that Fred and I, clamoring for its purchase, left Mother little to do except buy it. Once purchased, however, the wondrous volume remained unopened. It added to our library, however, a degree of class not offered by the books of the Holmes lady, and Fred and I were always sure to see, when company was to come, that the book had a place on the front-room table where no eye could miss it.

During the latter weeks of summer we were called upon by a photographer traveling with a light wagon bearing a light-proof space into which he could retreat when his labors or sleep might overtake him. A large case, with lock, was filled with plates, and on hand were printing equipment and chemicals called for by his trade.

Personable and tactful, the young man was gracious when Mother assured him that we, the entire O'Donnell family, were not artistically inclined, except Fred, who could manage the organ and play several pieces, including the "Blue Danube," although Tommy, even at his tender age, could play two or three chords. This with a smile at Fred and me, but from the visitor a glance of utter detestation.

These social amenities required so great a time that long shadows were arriving upon the eastern portion of the landscape. The situation reminded the caller of sleep, whereupon he broached skillfully the idea of a trade of a group picture for a night's lodging and meals. Mother, with a look that said of course we couldn't turn him out into the dark, agreed.

Compared with the peddlers the young man was a complete loss as a conversationalist. He was reticent in every department of information, in which our entire family was loquacious. We did learn that he came from out around St. John's, but since Father and Mother knew no one there, talk on that subject bogged down.

I now suspect that the photographer's want of interest in our wealth of conversational themes was due to worry about the late start he would get in the morning, since the sun would have to be well up in the skies before he could take a picture and develop the negative. Moreover, the day might be so cloudy and dull that a picture could not be taken.

> ...he lifted from a bag a huge volume which, he declared, gave a true and exciting account of the discovery and rescue of Doctor Livingston by James Gordon Bennett. "A book, Mrs. O'Donnell, that must be placed in the home of every red-blooded American!"

Sleep for me came late for thinking upon the visitor's problems. I mentioned my misgivings to Fred, who dismissed my fears with the interesting point that a young feller with a swell mustache like his always had plenty to worry about and so don't lose any sleep over it.

The photographer was away by eleven o'clock next day and by noon he would be at the Gibbses, where he would have dinner. Possibly too he would brighten considerably and progressively as he put more miles between him and the O'Donnell boys, who, the moment his back was turned, had looked his wagon over thoroughly, dingus after dingus, gizmo after gizmo, thingamabob after doohickey, affording prolonged speculation as to the functions of each.

Salesmen traveled the forests to seek out settlements, mills and industries which were founded by men whose foresight and genius started those enterprises.

It was months later, in winter, on a rainy night, that Father was awakened by a violent pounding on our front door. He arose and lit a lamp, which, through the vair-colored set of panes arranged in the door, told the visitor or visitors that their summons had been heard. By this time the two boys upstairs were looking in vain through windows to catch sight of possible visitors. When Father had modestly slipped into trousers, he answered the door and a young man stepped into the room out of the rain.

"I and a friend out in the cutter," we could hear the visitor saying, "are on our way home in Midland – Why George O'Donnell, you old—"

Father grasped an outstretched hand. "Frank Williams, what in heaven's name—I live here. This is my home, and—"

Frank explained about the dance in Shepherd and how they had furnished the music and had barely started for home when the storm came up.

"We've got to find a place to sleep. Could you—"

Father told him he had found the right place, and by the time he had gone back to the driveway and reached the stable he would be down to get his pony fixed up for the night.

In another twenty minutes the three of them were in the house and the young men had been introduced to Mother as young barbers in Midland who, one or the other of them, always cut Father's hair and trimmed his mustache and beard.

Mother already had tea things on and Fred and I, listening from our vantage point at the top of the stairs, became thrilled with the conversation. News was given Father of acquaintances and friends whom he had not seen in a coon's age, from Saginaw on the south to Averill and Sanford on the North.

In time conversation turned from people to dances, and Fred and I all but fell over the banister as we learned that at dances Frank played the banjo and Earl (we had not caught his last name) handled the autoharp.

"What's an autoharp?" I breathed excitedly to Fred, and his answer was that it was a lot like a flute only bigger. "We'll get a look at her in the morning," he added.

In the meantime, Father was managing the conversation so skillfully that he could ask why after all he and Mother couldn't hear them play a piece. They would be glad to, George, and soon sweet chords were making their dulcet way upstairs to Fred and me.

"It does like a flute, don't it?" I whispered. Fred, however, shifted the conversation to a subject with which he was more familiar.

"Listen—that's 'My Bunny Lays over the Ocean' they're playing now."

This air coming to an end, the musicians struck into what I took to be a schottische, a movement that I regarded with sheer enchantment. In my ecstasy I started to clap my hands, only to lose my balance and go rolling down the steps and into the front room.

I had not stopped rolling when Fred, who had tried in vain to stop me, followed, coming to a halt nearby but beating my distance by a good yard.

This contretemps brought to a halt the musical program, and after a fitting introduction of Fred and me, Father took the young men to their room. Their instruments were left exposed to Fred's and my gaze and when I had been assured by Father that the autoharp was not of the flute family, Fred and I declared a sudden passion for banjoes and autoharps.

Such was our devotion to the instruments that in the morning Father asked the visitors if they could not order for Fred a banjo, and for me an autoharp. They could, and they did, and Father on his next trip to Midland picked up the instruments, and by and by Fred and I were put into immediate operation, to the vast disquietude of women of the neighborhood who had accepted Mother's invitation to be dedicated to the sewing of carpet rags. Grandmother Nelson, of Cedar Lake, had bestowed upon Mother her carpet-making machine. It would arrive any day now and Mother, anxious to get going on a carpet, which of course we had no use for, was accumulating a supply of rags against the day when processing could begin.

Unfortunately Fred and I had not carried our studies of the two instruments beyond one or two simple chords. These we could never play twice alike. To the credit of the guests of the afternoon, it can be stated that their acquaintance with music was less than Fred's and mine and they greeted each of our contributions with "My sakes, ain't that just grand!" and, "Why, that is just beautiful, boys!" and similar encomiums. The same praises must have been expressed at the various supper tables that evening, for next morning we were waging intensive battles on a dozen different fronts, one after another, with the kids of the neighborhood. This was sufficient reward for having had the afternoon off and immediately we were clamoring for another carpet-rag shindig at our house.

Such an affair unhappily was far in the offing, but a few weeks later Mother discovered that Mrs. Gibbs owned a machine for sewing quilts. Could she borrow it? She could and did. Again the women folk of our vicinity were invited in, and Fred and I were to supply music for the occasion. Fred, when we went into a huddle on the affair, told me in strict confidence that he had resolved not to be a lumberjack but a banjoist in some cussed orchestra. When pressed, he allowed that a place might be found for me in the capacity of head autoharpist. Order was thus beginning to emerge from the chaos that hitherto had rendered dubious our future plans.

The quilting affair came off with greater éclat and more sugarcoated cookies than the carpet-rag bee had done. Next morning, however, the boys at school, by now violently fed up with their mother's ecstatic reports on our handling of musical programs, were waiting for us. Will Jones, who hitherto had always taken his side with us, was in charge of the mob.

Normal mornings the boys arrived at school a half hour or so ahead of the nine o'clock bell: now they apparently had been there all night. John Wilsey had been chosen to open the fracas with a healthy punch, with no preliminary stuff, in the general direction of my right eye. The blow succeeded in reaching my chin. The insult offending me was taken up by Fred, who waded in to brush John Wilsey aside, only to run afoul of Will Jones, who up and landed a blow over Fred's right eye.

The battle was on, in the ratio of seven boys against two. That meant six against Fred, since John and I, with our style of battling, could well be at it all forenoon unless stopped by our teacher, which seemed unlikely. In due time Fred, overpowered, was picked up, kicking and squirming, and carried to Black Creek and dropped off the bridge. Over across the road from the school, John and I were still clawing at each other when the final bell sounded. John dropped his mitts, as did I getting, the two of us inside in time by the skin of our teeth.

Jennie Birch, our teacher, was so right when she told Mother one time that it was a pleasure to teach at our school: the boys were so eternally fighting among themselves that they had no time or thought to turn upon her.

Chapter Nine

The Joneses

© R.P. Nadeau

LIFE IN A NORTH WOODS LUMBER CAMP

The previous May, Father had told Fred and me that during the summer we would be having some new children to play with. Particularly he spoke of the Jones family. It seems that Alex Jones, one of our teamsters the previous winter, had decided to buy a piece of land nearby, put up a house and bring his family in. This news did not thrill us because all of the previous season in camp Alex had been forever harping on Will and Nora, his children. It was Will this and Nora that, until we were thoroughly fed up on the subject.

Fred and I had several conversations dealing with the project, and we decided thoroughly to dislike the children, when Fred, telling Father about it, went off on a new track.

"I bet you don't talk all the time about us to other folks like he does about hizzen!"

When Father replied that it was all he ever did talk about, we decided that probably fathers couldn't help it. When Will and Nora did arrive, we accepted them with little enthusiasm and with a trace of reserve in our manner.

The family moved into a story-and-a-half

log house a half mile over across Potter Creek that Alex had built. They arrived in the middle of an afternoon, and Mother sent Fred and me to ask the family for supper with us.

The July day was hot and stuffy. Fred and I had been going barefoot, a condition of undress that would not do for so fashionable an occasion. Fred and I got togged up so quickly that Mother was astonished when she heard the screen door latch behind us, only to become convulsed with laughter at the get-up of her two gallants as they set out in glory. Fred was wearing his winter felts and rubbers, his great pride and joy, and I the copper-toed boots that Santa Claus had brought me for Christmas, neither of us with socks. The rest of us were pretty much as we had been all day, I in a scanty panty waist with abbreviated pants buttoned on, and Fred without benefit of shirt and in long trousers held up by red galluses.

Determined upon making an impression in spite of Mother's hilarity, we went on, and in single file, an idea that Fred had picked up from a story he had read in the Midland Sun about Indians on the warpath.

As we neared the Jones house, we had stopped to get the lay of the land when I startled Fred by giving our "holo-ho-lo-lo" call—a frightening routine that we had worked out. The call had the effect of bringing the Jones children to the door and looking out upon us in stark terror.

For our part, Fred and I came on, cautiously now, a few steps at a time, until we had reached a pine stump, a dozen yards from the house. Upon the stump we rested our elbows, chins in cupped hands, staring steelily at the newcomers. Fred was sizing up Will, meditating upon how very much he would like to drop a right under his left jaw, and I was lost in wonder at the vision of sheer loveliness presented by Nora, near my own age—pensive blue eyes that matched a little blue dress, black hair hanging in ringlets—in every way, I felt, a creature for a kid of my age to lose his head about.

Our position behind the stump had the disadvantage of concealing our footgear from the view of the very persons we had meant to impress. This defect Fred corrected by moving stealthily from behind our barricade and toward the doorway, I just behind him. We came up close and stopped, Fred volunteering a reserved "Hello, Will!" Will returned the greeting with an enthusiastic "Uh-huh," and Fred coming back with a smart, "I'm Fred."

In the meantime, my enchantment knowing no bounds, I went straight up to Nora, pecked her upon the lips and said, "Damn you!" This was a trick I had tried out on Aunt Jenny Bell in Saginaw the previous winter, and with such success that I took it on as a regular procedure.

Our foot coverings had made so little impression that we could as well have come barefoot. Fred tried to correct the defect by suddenly jabbing the toe of his right foot into the sand and, his hands behind him, swinging his body half-way around and back again, and so on through a half dozen semi-gyrations.

This was completely lost on our audience, when presently the parents came to the door. Alex beamed. "Why, if it ain't Fred and Tom, Edith!" Edith said she was glad to see us, dears, and suddenly was aware of our accoutrements as respected especially our feet. Clapping a hand to her mouth she turned quickly and went inside, with cries of "Oh my, oh my!" between shrieks of laughter.

In some way we got Mother's invitation through, and Fred and I turned and trudged home, and when an hour later the family showed up at the house my delight was ecstatic. Things were already laid out on the table and Mother soon had shown off Marie and Myrtle to Edith. The two men were supplying a subdued background of chatter, asking about each other's health for the tenth time, and I, standing at a meager attention, stared my soul out at Nora.

The Wilsey family came in before the summer was out, and although John, nearly my age, had his points, it was the Jones children mostly who shared our fun. We were practically inseparable, except when I was helping to keep the Wilsey mill running. Often Will and Nora stayed all night at our house. On such occasions Fred and Will slept together, and I was inconsolable when Mother refused to let me sleep with Nora, insisting instead that the honor should go to Marie.

Jake Wilsey, who had not worked for Father, had come in with a

sawmill from out around Pleasant Valley and set up business on Spring Creek, a small stream a mile south and west of our camp. From the moment the outfit began turning out lumber, mine was a split personality. Without apparent loss of any of

my devotion to my dream girl, I became a sawmill addict. John, Jake's kid, from the start took me on as a pupil in the finer arts of running a mill. He had, I rather felt, a one-track mind, for he never yielded to the blandishment of my rollways and log jams, as I enlarged upon them, but any time of day he could be found hanging around his father's mill.

John was primarily a setter, although there was nothing, he confided to me, that he couldn't do around the shebang. To be a setter was tops with me, for it meant riding back and forth on the long carriage with the log that was being cut into sweet-smelling boards by the huge circular saw. On each return of the carriage from the saw, just move the log over another board's thickness, pull a lever and zip! The saw was at it again.

For the first step in my education I was to sit on a pile of boards nearby and observe, goggle-eyed, the expert quality of John's setting. This went on for a week, when one morning my mentor, sensing that I had mastered this first step, let me stand on the carriage, just back of him. This went on for a dozen or so sessions when one day I was permitted to handle the lever that sent the carriage rolling up to the saw. Then came a day when I was to send my first log into and through the saw alone! John gave me some last-minute instructions, and at long last told me to let her slide.

I pulled a lever, we moved, and after what seemed years the saw was screaming its way through the log; a board dropped—my board! Tremblingly I reversed the lever and we shot back to the place of starting. John wanted me to do it again, but the excitement had tuckered me out and I threw myself onto a pile of sawdust, if possible to regain even a portion of my sapped energies.

In good time John initiated me into the mysteries of the boiler room. The Wilsey boiler room was so called because the boiler and engine were the only parts of the mill with a roof over them. John, never too technical about details, added a new word to my under-worked vocabulary: "This dingus here is to tell you how much water's in the boiler!" He pointed to a gauge, which didn't excite me half as much as the discovery that you had to have water in a boiler. John next put his hand on a valve, giving it a twist. "This dingus," he informed me, "brings water from the creek."

As so it went, dingus after dingus. I never did learn the names of half the gadgets that stuck out all over the place, although over the next two or three years, what with this and other mills that started up nearby, I became able to tend a boil-along with a fair degree of success. No boiler ever exploded on me, and that was something, considering the state of most of the equipment that was brought into the woods.

Jake Wilsey did not himself traffic in lumber. He sawed for others, and Father was by far his best customer. As a matter of fact, Father later on kept the mill busy over one or two years, feeding into it many hundreds of thousands of feet of logs and hauling the lumber to markets in Shepherd and Mount Pleasant.

Of the new arrivals that summer, Bud and True Hodgins gave me perhaps my gravest concern. They were twins, the first I had ever heard of. Moreover, their birthday was the same as mine, although they were a year older than I. These facts gave me a good deal to think about. Even if they were twins, they looked alike, in a two-peas-in-a-pod kind of way, and in no way showed any abnormal tendencies.

I carried the problem to Nora, but from her got little help. She accepted the entire arrangement without show of alarm. To her twins was just one of those things that you had or you hadn't. Brazenly she told me one day that sometime she was going to have twins, and when I had recovered from my surprise she added, "And then after that I'm going to have three of them all at one, like Mrs. Tanner, who used to live across the road from us."

In my dither over this confession, I consulted Fred, who told me that hell, you could have as many damn children as you wanted. "You could even have three to onct," he said. "Somebody had three down in Riverdale one time!"

Chapter Ten

Such Goings On

© R.P. Nadeau

LIFE IN A NORTH WOODS LUMBER CAMP

IT HAD BEEN the previous autumn, at the beginning of our second lumbering season, that Pete Murray, keeping a promise made to Father, joined the crew. Considering the effects on camp morale, the announcement could have been regarded as a threat.

Peter expected, and was given, no favors because of previous associations with Father. He took his place among the winter's hands, and without so much as a word in the shanties as to the previous friendship between the two men. He found his companions younger, some by several years, than himself, but such was his energy, his love of fun and mischief, the robust part he played in all shanty didoes, that except for his graying hair he could have passed for the youngest of the lot.

Ideas, that was Pete's long suit, and his first inspiration came when, glancing at the oats bin in a corner of the barn, he asked why in heaven's name, to save ground-floor space and time, George didn't put the bin up in the gables. Put it there and a chute would bring the oats tumbling down as you needed them, and in a jiffy.

Father asked how in heck the oats would be got up and into the bin and Pete was ready with the answer.

"It would be easy, George. When a load comes in jest run the bags up with a block and tackle. A feller standin' up there would empty the bag into the bin, and the chute would bring the oats tumbling into a barrel here right in front of the horses' noses!"

All of this Father not only assented to but carried out. The arrangement, if not an improvement, yet was more picturesque in operation than having the big bin at the bottom. As it turned out, it gave life a joyous touch for Fred and me. Immediately Fred was raising himself, arm over arm, and then, in reverse detail, lowering himself to the ground. And more, he was constantly bringing in kids from here and there to witness his skill, they in turn clamoring for a try.

For the younger fry, the block and tackle routine was an introduction to shambles, Fred and I resisting the temptation to caution them to put the left arm around the end of the rope having a noose for the foot. Failure to do this would, upon the first pull at the rope, send the foot shooting out into space in the general direction of Potter Creek, as Fred explained to me upon my first attempt at the joyous sport. A fall from a height of two, three, or four feet would send a kid falling on his back and howling in pain.

When the last kid in the neighborhood had been initiated, Pete took over. He started with Father, and when mayhem immediately struck, Pete was broken and contrite. Fortunately, Father was barely off the floor when he fell on his back, but the glance that he gave Pete was tinged with fire and brimstone. Before he could threaten Pete with immediate and complete annihilation, however, the two old friends were all but shedding tears and their friendship came through intact.

Pete's genius extended into the financial field, introducing Fred and me to a deal that somehow we had overlooked; Fred afterwards told me that at first he suspected something snide about it, but Pete was Father's friend and who was he to pass judgment?

A man with a shingle mill had bought the timber in a cedar swamp a mile from our camp. Eight or nine houses had been run up for the families of the shingle weavers and the mill now was in operation.

The ladies of the mill pleaded with Mother to supply them with milk, and in the discussions that followed at our end a decision was reached to let the ladies have their way, the milk each morning to be delivered by Fred and me. The price was fixed at five cents a quart.

Pete, when we reported the matter to him, was all sympathy for the two milkmen and immediately went into what he always called a left-handed huddle with himself. A day elapsed and Pete then announced a new and epochal plan.

"See here, Freddie, le's see can't we make some money for you and Tom. It'd be easy. Your ma decided to sell the milk for five cents. Now you buy it from her at five cents and sell it at six cents. The hull deal to be 'tween you and the wimmin at the mill." Mother would furnish the pails and Fred and I the footwork.

Fred put the business before Mother and she thought it would be a pleasant arrangement. Deliveries began two days later. A dozen quarts and more each day were delivered, and Fred and I cleaned up on the deal. Unfortunately there was no way, short of starting a store, to squander our loot. We encouraged Father to take us with him on trips to Shepherd and Midland, and what with pop and chewing gum and candy, our cash in hand for Christmas presents soon was practically nonexistent. A year later the cedar timber had all been converted into shingles and the mill was removed to Shepherd.

Pete's most devastating effect on my own habits came one day when I found him smoking a dried elm root. This form of debauchery was not to be sneezed at, I told myself: Elm windfalls along our creek bottoms were common. The roots of these upturned trees, when they had become free of clinging soil and suns and winds had dried the roots, were easy on the draw, Pete told me. I was growing on six years of age and maybe it was time I began to train to be a sawyer and grow up big and tall like my father.

No sooner thought than done, and next day I came in with the men at evening with a lighted root between my lips and emitting a cloud of smoke. Mother was shocked, she afterwards told me, and had to suppress a smile and an impulse to take me over her knee. By no word or look, however, did she let on that suddenly she had observed that here was a new man in her midst.

A half year of this and I began wheedling tobacco from our jacks. The response was overwhelming, and in a short time I had added chewing tobacco, only used, however, at such times as I had a pipe in my mouth. Determined that my vices would not affect the supply of tobacco, which Fred handed out and charged to the men, I borrowed from Emory Lewis and others of our shanties.

I was headed for perdition, a point at which I might have arrived only too soon, when Nora Jones moved in and told me... she would never marry a man who smoked. That was it. I threw away, into Potter Creek... the beauteous pipe carved for me by Skinny Perry from an elm burl.

I was headed for perdition, a point at which I might have arrived only too soon, when Nora Jones moved in and told me, amid a cloud of Jolly Tar which George Kent had cut up with a knife, how she could never marry a man who smoked. That was it. I threw away, into Potter Creek, which we were crossing, the beauteous pipe carved for me by Skinny Perry from an elm burl.

It was Skinny, I may add, not Pete, who got Father into the literary racket. The Midland Sun came each week to our house, eventually finding its way to the shanties for the education of such as could read. Skinny, when fed up on the correspondence items from around the county, wondered why Father didn't send in pieces from our part of Greendale. "Show'm how to write, George!"

On his first trip to Midland, Father went into a huddle with the editor. The editor, thus made aware of his derelictions, asked Father to take on the job and from that day on no incident was too trivial, no figure too humble, not to be given a place in the Sun. Literary style in our reports might have its ups and downs, but any shortcomings in grammar or syntax would be because Fred, always overworked by play, too often composed the week's stint.

It was in the autumn of 1888 that Father's genius in extracurricular affairs was seen to best advantage. The presidential campaign was on

Bark peeling was the main job in the woods. The hemlock bark was taken to tanneries for the tanning of leather. The best hemlock logs were sawed into lumber for local building.

COURTESY OF GEORGE SHAUGHNESSY

and had reached what for our sector was a feverish pitch. Father was an over-heated Democrat; Mother, hailing from a race of rabid Republicans, sat out each political campaign. Her tolerance was undoubtedly due to the fact that all issues, on both sides, took a bad beating in political debate. So it was when Fred asked why couldn't we have a political rally? The suggestion was received with acclamation by Father.

Father appointed a committee from the local folk, a date was set, and Father engaged himself to secure a speaker who would tell the Republicans off.

The committee's chairman was Jim Green, who had come in with his family from Tennessee and lived in a shanty of sorts a mile to the south. Fred suggested to Jim the thought of having refreshments for the crowd, an idea that was received with enthusiasm by the chairman, whose family larder might consist at any time of a mess of shiners that Jim would bring in towards evening, in summer a dish of wild raspberries, and a quantity of biscuits limited always by the amount of flour in the cupboard. To Mother, then, Jim would hand the job of preparing food for the rally.

Our men had arrived in camp by this time, and when word reached them of the impending rally they accounted themselves, to a man, as ardent supporters of Benjamin Harrison. They would be on hand for the refreshments and would behave throughout like gentlemen; they had respect for George O'Donnell's political convictions, but their minds were made up!

Everybody came out, each in his best bib and tucker. Fred had prevailed upon Mother to have the refreshments before the meeting, as a stimulant to enthusiasm. The results of the arrangement were devastating. Our jacks, the eating over, returned in a body to the shanties to resume interrupted games of big casino; members of the committee, sitting bolt upright and without the slightest expression in their eyes, were all there, with wives and offspring; Miss Sweeting, who was visiting Mother, looked sweet, as did my Nora. Our part of Greendale never had invalids, so that only the infants of the community, and a necessary nurse or two, were missing.

The speaker on the rostrum seemed, as he surveyed the audience, exceedingly depressed. Had his mood had the power of determining the result of the election, Father told us next morning, Jut Gannon could easily be our next president. This view of Father's was passed on to Emory Lewis next morning and he, to give Jut an early start, put the matter to a vote of the two shanties, and without a dissenting vote he was elected to the exalted office of President of the United States.

Chapter Eleven

North America Nine Million

© R.P. Nadeau

LIFE IN A NORTH WOODS LUMBER CAMP

EARLY IN THE AUTUMN, Mother reported to Fred that the coming winter would be spent by him in Cedar Lake. Object? Some needed schooling. "Yes, Fred, they have a wonderful school there and you will live with Grandma and Grandpa Nelson!"

To Mother's amazed surprise, Fred offered no objection. He was devoted, with the rest of us, to our grandparents. The old gentleman, a lawyer, had been Circuit Court Judge, and in spite of step-grandchildren being out of his line he seemed completely sold on us. And because Grandma Nelson was Mother's mother, she was something kind of special.

"You don't make up your mind whether you like Grandma or not," Fred confided to me one time. "You just like her. She's nicer even than Mrs. Gibbs."

This high opinion of Mrs. Gibbs came as a revelation to me. Mrs. Gibbs was the Mrs. Gibbs of the Gibbs neighborhood. It was beyond me that she could be compared with anyone. Then it all came to me:

"I betcha wouldn't say that if Mrs. Gibbs didn't have an ice cream freezer!"

What might have developed into one of

our interminable arguments was brought to a halt when Fred reminded me that Grandma Nelson also had an ice cream freezer.

Mother was really concerned lest her children grow up "like—like stone-rollers," as she told Father one time.

Mother had somehow become stone-roller conscious. We had discovered a dozen or more of them lying in a Salt River riffle a half mile east of our house. Always they were nudging pebbles here and there with no apparent reason. Mother's thought was, it seems clear, that if with a fine mind like Fred's you wished only to shunt things here and there you were in the same category with Old Pat.

It was at that point that Old John Bugbee came to our attention when Fred announced at dinner one night that Old John had been at the Oliver Haights, down in the Gibbs neighborhood, two or three nights ago holding a geography school.

The news fell on deaf ears. No one asked who Old John Bugbee was, and I was about to ask the question myself when Fred explained.

"They say he's a pussy little feller, in a bearskin cap and muttonchop whiskers and comes to your house and holds a geography school and limps."

That did it. Mother was all interest. Old Man Bugbee might hold the answer to a problem she had. If he could hold a geography school why not a penmanship school and a reading school, and an orthography school? Orthography in those days was a must in just about anybody's curriculum.

Mother learned quickly why Old John's list of topics for educational projects was necessarily restricted. She got it from Mrs. Haight, who passed by that morning on her way to Shepherd to visit her cousin Elida.

"He don't teach you," said Mrs. Haight. "He jest gets you to singin' about Roosha and the Amazonic River and things like that. It's real nice fun. We had our parlor full and part of the kitchen and Oliver and the Brokaw boys sloppin' over into the kitchen," a statement that was far short of saying what Mother thought Mrs. Haight meant by it. "The only trouble is you have to have him come to supper and stay all night and give him his breakfast in the morning, and perviding he goes…"

She paused as a hurt look came into her eyes.

"The fact is," she presently resumed, "he's with us yet and we don't know any ways to get shet of him."

Fred had the answer. "Can't we have him, Ma?" He added that we could have all the kids in and they're dying to learn about Roosha.

While Mother pondered this one, Mrs. Haight said she hoped it would be real soon. Mother replied to the extent of saying that she would see.

Immediately Mrs. Haight said a hurried good-bye, dashed to the road to untie her horse from the hitching post, turned about and headed for home.

Within a couple of hours Old John turned up in person. Mother, astonished, suspected that Mrs. Haight, to expedite matters, had driven him to the edge of the clearing, discharged her passenger, and then hurried home.

It was strange that we hadn't heard about Old John before. He lived, after a fashion, over around the 'Valley,' as Pleasant Valley was called by people in a hurry. That would be some six miles south of our camp. It seems that he had appropriated for his uses a log shack that somebody had vacated. Here he lived alone, and had it not been for the comic aspect presented by his long mutton-chop whiskers, his pussiness, and a disarming pair of sharp, bead-like eyes, people would have called him a hermit, with children running breathlessly past his house at night. He was sixty, maybe sixty-five, years old and wore a faded gray checkered suit that made you think of the cartoons of Boss Tweed.

It was too late to assemble the neighborhood that night, but Mother decided that it could be worked out for the next evening. Fred and I of course would see that the neighborhood was notified of the great social event, wherefore bright and early next morning we were up and about and by ten o'clock the tidings had been heralded out as far as the Harts and the Parsonses. Nobody was ever dated up for anything, and everybody always hankered for a whirl at any project that held promise of breaking the monotony of staying at home.

The hour was set for seven o'clock. An early supper over, Fred and I cleared the long dining room of unnecessary furniture, set up all available chairs, and brought benches from the shanties. Our efforts were supported by John Wilsey and others of the younger fry, who, in their thirst for knowledge, were showing up hours in advance of their elders.

All afternoon Old John Bugbee was kept in wraps out of sight. He must make a dramatic entrance. Father, in Midland on business, could not preside, a function that was taken over by Mother. By seven o'clock the room was crowded, all in eager anticipation.

Presently Mother entered from the living-room, took a place in front of the audience, and made clear how happy she was that they had come; it showed how interested the neighborhood was in things of the mind. She was certain they would be especially interested in the marvelous program to be offered by Mr. John Bugbee.

This was a signal for John to emerge from his seclusion and to acknowledge the applause that greeted his entrance. The long, low sweeping bow with which again and again he acknowledged the greeting of the audience out front only brought on renewed applause, but fascination finally gave way to curiosity as to what his spiel held for them, and school was able to get under way.

Old John's first contribution was a little prelude, which he had thought up:

> Sing ho, sing hi, sing hey,
> Something new starts every day!

To say that this was sung is something of an exaggeration. Old John had little sense of key and the only respect in which the program was of a musical nature lay in the fact that Old John was all over the tonal map.

The audience was too awed to applaud. The performer then took from his pocket an impressive-looking dingus which Fred whispered to me was a tuning fork. Holding it at arm's length and getting us ready for action, Old John went off on an entirely fresh tack.

"First," he told us, "I have arranged, to a tune you will all recognize, the five great continents and the size of each one. Then there will be a song about rivers, and the countries of the world and their capitals, and songs about the oceans and islands."

Our performer, after catching his breath, tapping his tuning fork on the stove, again suddenly went off in a different key as he set forth in an unearthly tune, upon the affecting lyric:

> North America nine million,
> North America nine million.
>
> South America seven million,
> South America seven million.
>
> Af-ree-cah twelve million,
> Af-ree-cah twelve million.
> A-zi-ah seventeen million,
>   Largest of the five grand divisions;

A-zi-ah seventeen million,
  Largest of the five grand divisions.

Eu-rope four million,
  Smallest of the five grand divisions;
Eu-rope four million,
  Smallest of the five grand divisions.

The trick in the melody, decidedly a sing-song affair, was, for the achievement of a fine cadence, to raise each underscored syllable a half dozen notes and give it an extra amount of oomph. A breath-taking climax was led up to in the third stanza by giving the "ah" a double dose of emphasis, reaching high into the upper registers for a suitable note for purposes of accentuation. Coming to the final stanza, we really cooked with gas, climbing an even octave to get at the "rope," which was held onto for ten seconds or so, then picking up the rest of the passage and letting nature take its course.

The song was sung and resung and when the professor was satisfied with our effort the next song, dealing with the great rivers of the world, was taken up and soon Rock, our favorite dog, decided to add to the cacophony, and with results so successful that John, deeply shaken, could not go on. With masterful control of his emotions, he declared that his school was a serious business and they would understand that the rest of the program would have to await another occasion. With this, he beat a retreat into the sitting room, where he sat alone, nursing his wounded spirit.

The hour being young, somebody suggested dancing. Emory Lewis, the best fiddler in the shanties, fetched his instrument; the floor was cleared and two sets were filled up. With Alex Jones calling off, we had one of the sprightliest hoe-downs of the season. Education for the children had made a start, but its full flowering must await another day.

Chapter Twelve

"Mon" Lost in the Woods

© R.P. Nadeau

LIFE IN A
NORTH WOODS
LUMBER CAMP

AROUND EIGHT O'CLOCK one October evening, before he turned in, Old Pat Moran laid down the last stick of shavings for the morning fire and went down to the stable for a final time thinking something might have been overlooked.

While closing the double doors he suddenly stopped dead in his tracks when a faint sound of a rifle shot reached his ears.

The old warrior suddenly sprang into action and rushed to our house, his hand trembling as he shook his cane upon finding Father.

"There's a mon lost, George!
I hear'n his gun!"

A gunshot at night was a sure sign that someone out in the woods needed help. The household was suddenly electrified at the news, as was the lumber shanty below the house as quickly as Father could get down with the news.

Presently the jacks gathered on our porch. Father directed the searchers to concentrate on the east and north sides, reasoning properly that men could not easily get lost in the land to the south or to the west.

Ben Watson, who this season had been

taken off the list of sawyers and made a swamper, was for everybody setting off in different directions, the women folks of course excepted. He was certain that by climbing trees and yelling at the top of our voices someone would be sure to make contact with whoever was lost out there in the night.

Father suggested that it would be best to first fire a salvo from our double-barrel shotgun. The roar hardly died away when a faint report came from afar off, easterly.

"They hear'n us!" Jut Gannon declared.

Everybody agreed except my brother Fred. "How do you know?" he asked. "Maybe he didn't hear you at all, Pa."

At that point Mother broke in, "What direction did it come from?"

Discussion indicated that the report came from several directions. The men decided to strike out in pairs, in various directions. Emory Lewis would carry Old Bet on his shoulder for future soundings.

Just as the rescuers began to filter out, Dave Wright dashed in asking if anybody had seen his old man, who had gone out hunting birds that morning in the region east of the O'Donnellses.

My emotions were not unmixed. I harbored certain prejudices toward Old Man Wright. He was a short, stocky man, proud of his bulging paunch. Mutton-chop whiskers without a mustache adorned his face.

All the kids called him "Pussy." Pussy liked to tease us in a not-so-friendly way.

Suddenly another report of gunfire reached us. "That's old Bet," Fred declared. "It's coming from over at the Cedar Swamp northeast."

Then came another and another followed by an answering shot. Within minutes, from various directions there began to be heard the calls of our men, who, from tops of trees, would be cupping their mouths with their hands and letting go with a hair-raising "Hoo-oo-oo-oo!"

Meantime Dave Wright was declaring, "Pop was never lost before."

"Howjuh know? Ever ask him?" My brother wanted to know.

Presently another shot was heard. Evidently impatient, Pussy was going away from the rescuers.

"Now he's getting rattled," declared Father. "He'll never stay in one place and let the men come to him. No. He's got to dash around and find them!"

Ten minutes later more shots showed that he was moving farther away and veering to the south.

Bert Stahl and Emory Lewis had gone across the river and struck into the timber when they caught the report of Pussy's firearm. The two soon closed in and at long last had their man, safe and sound, back at our camp.

Pussy's troubles, as we gathered from his story of high night-time adventure, lay in

In the early days of logging, man power and horses were the only power used.

COURTESY OF JOHN DONAHUE

too great a trust in signs. He had a vast distrust of compasses. "Wouldn't have one of the cussed things in my house!" He had an unwavering belief in his ability to guide himself by phenomena like moss on the side of a tree and by the heavenly bodies. Unfortunately the day had been overcast and the sun and stars had failed him. When he found that it was time to take himself home it came over him that he was lost. Dashing this way and that for a tree bearing a coating of moss, he saw darkness come on and soon the blackout complete in the forest.

> **He had a vast distrust of compasses. "Wouldn't have one of the cussed things in my house!" He had an unwavering belief in his ability to guide himself by phenomena like moss on the side of a tree and by the heavenly bodies.**

Pussy was easily the outstanding brunt of many jokes. Father, anxious to make up on his lost hours of sleep, called the entire assemblage to our front stoop. In his thanks for their help, he gave a dubious glance at Pussy and ordered Old Pat to let the shanty boys sleep until six o'clock. The camp hands looked stunned in their thanks. Only Mother smiled. It was Saturday night!

Chapter Thirteen

Cupid Could Just as Well Have Stayed Home

© R.P. Nadeau

LIFE IN A
NORTH WOODS
LUMBER CAMP

CUPID NEVER got really going in our section of Greendale. In the nearly eight years that we remained there, the number of weddings that occurred could be counted on the fingers of Jim Hodgins' right hand, from which the two fingers next to the thumb had been clipped off by knot-saws in shingle mills.

No heart of a proper age but could be made to beat a little faster, of course, given the appearance of a comely girl or a lad with a way about him. As for anyone going off the deep end and getting spliced, however, this was not for Greendale.

Our hired girls, and the schoolteachers who boarded at our house, were the chief objects of such male attentions as were aroused. By June, the month sacred to love, our men, the schoolteachers, and all except one of our hired girls, had gone out of the woods. Arnie, of all our hired girls, had the summer spot; Jut Gannon was sweet on Arnie, but his more tender sentiments were of the here-today-and-gone-tomorrow kind.

Had even occasional and mild flutterings of the heart been stirred in our immediate camp, the house had not been planned with

an eye out for sparking conveniences. The living room was none too large and into it, from adjoining bedrooms, came frequent yowlings of Marie and Myrtle, and not infrequently the goings-on of both of them at once. This left only the kitchen, and Pat, in his room just beyond the cook-stove, did just about everything to discourage any current equivalent of necking except burn down the house. Not that Pat was against the idea of love in principle; his concern was entirely for the wood box behind the stove, filled with the precious pine kindling for next morning's uses, which he had so laboriously split and decorated with fancy shaving effects.

George Kent one day snapped out of the immense indifference that the region displayed toward the more gentle emotions, and heavily dated Mattie Hickling, our schoolteacher for the winter. That night George let himself into the kitchen just as the rest of the men were getting into their bunks. Already the family were in the arms of Morpheus, as Fred was explaining to Will Cunningham next day.

Mattie let George in, and after the preliminary greetings silence ensued, broken only by what Pat could make out to be ill-suppressed giggles and soft whisperings. Something or other suggested to the couple the desirability of still more heat, and presently Pat heard the stove lid being moved, presenting in Pat's imagination a vision of his kindling going into the stove and on up in flames. He muttered a "dom" or two and twisted audibly in his bed as a sly hint.

When a quarter of an hour had passed, the stove lid again gave off sounds and again Pat repeated the hints. A third time Pat could hear George fussing with the stove, and this was it. Unable to endure further agony, Pat gave the Moran version of a leap from bed and, with his best limp, brandishing his cane wildly about, he suddenly appeared before the astonished lovers in his red longies and gave George a going over with his cane. Mattie unsnuggled herself from her boyfriend's arms just in time to see the rugged lover receiving healthy blows that rained right and left. So furious was the onslaught that George dashed for the door and was down and in his bunk by the time Mattie had swept out of the kitchen and gone into hers.

Fred and I were of little help in the general situation. One summer a lovely cousin of Mother's visited us, and swains from the Gibbs neighborhood began to swarm about. That was the summer of our first potato plantings, just after we had begun to dig new tubers for the table. The small ones left on the ground were fairly made for missiles for Fred and me. Our pockets were always filled with them, and one afternoon Sherm Baker, from the Wilsey mill, and Clara were cozily seated on one end of the front porch, their backs to us as we peered around a corner of the house. Without announcement we loosed a bombardment of potatoes, dodging out of sight with each volley. The effort was successful, and a half-hour later Sherm said well, he guessed he would have to go now.

Thereafter, it was enough for any young man in summer to show up at the house with a "sparkin'" look in his eye to send Fred and me to the potato patch. Did the couple go for a walk in the woods, Fred and I pelted them from behind trees; if they sought refuge in the dining room, we were concealed behind doors. It was all pretty discouraging to Cupid.

The younger element could take affairs of the heart or leave them. My own attachment for Nora was, of course, the real thing, and was so taken, I was sure by one and all. No winter was complete without at least two or three parties being held in each of our homes. These were strictly junior affairs and were given over almost entirely to kissing games.

Spin the plate, post office and snap and catch 'em were our favorites. I liked snap and catch 'em best of all because, it being faster, you got a greater volume of kisses for the evening's take. In this game you always selected your victim. I invariably chose Nora, and I in turn was selected by her. I was always in a state of dither and never missed a party. The other boys did not specialize, and if a girl after a party was going home their way okay, they'd walk with her; otherwise she'd have to hoof it alone, or with others who might be going in her direction.

Even the dances seemed powerless to create a sustained love interest in all except Nora and me. These were a rather regular Saturday night event held at our house. They bore essentially a homey touch, mostly got up as they were for our men and the hired girls. The people of the neighborhood knew that they were welcome and most of them would turn up. At any time during the winter, however, there were enough women at the house to fill up a set, and sometimes two sets, for square dancing.

The problem of music was a simple one after the banjo and autoharp came to us. Fred had soon picked up a few of the current dancing numbers for his banjo and helped me achieve the two or three chords afforded by a four-bar autoharp. The organ, however, always appealed to me as an accompanying instrument, and in this field my efforts were as unsavory as my efforts on the autoharp.

Fred and I had a marked degree of versatility. Let us at any time feel that we were getting into a rut, and Fred would work on my precious autoharp and I take over his banjo. If in other hours Father was in a mood to join us, he handled the violin and Mother, if importuned, would manipulate our reed organ. The four of us were regarded with no little envy by such neighbors as had no feeling for music and to whom volume was the complete and final end of music.

At any dance, of course, somebody had to call off. So long as our men were in camp, the job was competently handled. As more and more families moved into the area, almost always a man could be found to lend a hand. If things came to the worst, Fred could play the banjo and at the same time call off. On one or two occasions even I laid the autoharp aside and did the job, performances that earned me no laurels.

Visits of Mother's cousins from out around Ithaca called for more high-falutin' performances than we were accustomed to. Dances at these times were strictly in the special events class, and for them Father brought Will Hitzman from the Gibbs neighborhood. Will was easily the best fiddler for miles around. You had to hand it to Will for high-toned playing, despite the fact that being brought in from the outside was a grievous reflection on our own techniques.

It was one of these visits that brought the schottische to Greendale. Lily and Frank Brooke, from Ithaca, out where they played stylish card games like whist instead of double pedro and big casino, were all excited about the schottische, and Will Hitzman, having learned two

The only liquor ever seen in camp, we were so home-like in all ways, would be when some of the men coming into camp in early fall, and returning from a trip home at Christmas, toted a quart bottle or two in their turkey.

or three numbers, the pair put on an exhibition, stirring little interest in me, however—I who, by the time I had mastered the schottische, discovered that the two-step or something had become all the rage.

Saturday night dances continued up to the spring drive. As sure signs of the spring breakup appeared, such of the men as intended to take part in the drive began driving calks in their high river shoes, wherefore the floor soon became pock-marked.

How the men were able to dance in their calked shoes must remain a mystery. The calks made a sharp, crackling sound as they sank into the floor under the weight of the dancer, and again as they were pulled out, dragging tiny splinters from the boards as the dancers carried on, step after step. The calks of four or eight pairs of shoes were able fairly to drown out the music, and mornings after the dance you got splinters in your feet if you tried to walk barefoot over the desiccated floor.

The decorum of our dances made Fred and me feel sometimes that something must be missing. In the shanties we heard lumberjacks talk of dances up in the Tittebewass country, or over on the Muskegon—dances that were dances, stories that convinced you that the real purpose of parties was to get men lit up so that they could disembowel one another with knives or else shoot up the danged place with guns. It was never like that at our place. The only liquor ever seen in camp, we were so homelike in all ways, would be when some of the men coming into camp in early fall, and returning from a trip home at Christmas, toted a quart bottle or two in their turkey. From all reports, Fred and I gathered that drinking of gargantuan proportions was normal for our own jacks outside but that here—alas!—they let it alone.

Chapter Fourteen

Sky Pilot

RELIGION and religious observances in our operation had pretty much to shift for themselves. In the Gibbs schoolhouse, four miles away, Sunday-school sessions were held. Shepherd, eight miles to the south and west, had the usual small-village quota of religious denominations holding religious services.

In the Gibbs neighborhood, the problems of Sunday services were simple. The community was made up entirely of small farmers who had an attitude toward their immediate religious needs as clear as was their feeling toward civic obligations.

Except for our immediate family, the population was never a settled one. Our lumberjacks came from varied religious backgrounds and were in camp but a few months each year. None of our jacks had ever married or were interested in fraternal groups: It is clear that no institution pertaining to these interests could have claimed the interest of our men.

People of the Gibbs settlement, hailing to a man from "York State," remained New Yorkers in manner, speech and customs. Solid, upright folks who showed little interest in timber and timber operations, they viewed with a good

© R.P. Nadeau

LIFE IN A
NORTH WOODS
LUMBER CAMP

deal of amused tolerance the rather roisterous ways of our lumberjacks.

Just why the Gibbs families moved into this particular spot in the first place on the Black River, provided they were determined upon settlement in Greendale, was clear enough: They hit upon the largest area of arable land in the township. Land on the river bottoms produced good yields of oats and other grains, and back from the river were areas that could produce decent yields. Otherwise, the land around them was like the rest of Greendale: white sand that had no bottom until hardpan was reached, and hard might lie eight, ten feet and even more below the surface.

The Gibbs families formed the heart of the settlement, but in one way or another the other families were related to them. The head of the family was Truman, known far and wide as Old Man Gibbs—in the woods all men over say sixty years of age were Old Man This or Old Man That.

Truman had four sons: George, Frank, Will and Bert. These had each his own wife and brood and house on a plot of ground adjacent to Truman's farm. A piece down the road from Truman came the Brokaws, with their two sons, Jim and Manley, and next along the road, and a quarter-mile across the river were the Osborns, and back on the road were the Oliver Haights, and lastly Old Man Vorhees, with two sons, Jim and Casey. In our direction from Truman's home was Freeman Smith, who went in for onions exclusively, and a quarter mile further along the road was a family that seemed to get on well without signs of overexertion, the Goodwills.

Into the pattern of the Gibbs family were to be found a number of adopted and otherwise attached children, including Lennie Dean, a mischievous lad of near my own age; Ellen, a noble, white-browed woman who married Will Conrad, a riverman; and Nellie, who married Will Hitzman, a famous fiddler always being called upon to function at dances in a wide region.

The Gibbs home was the only frame house in the township, and the Gibbs schoolhouse the only other frame structure in the area.

Our lumberjacks, and the few families that had squatted in our vicinity, for no observable reason, were nomads in spirit, here in Greendale today and gone tomorrow. The lumberjacks up in Muskegon or Lapeer counties had the squatters in any spot offering a deserted shanty to move into. Mother's background was notably religious, but she knew the lumberjack and the nomad too well to be drawn into any attempt to minister to their spiritual needs.

For the sake of any reputation for godliness which Greendale might wish to achieve, the Gibbs neighborhood could always be pointed to with pride. This can be said in spite of what happened to Ben Ball. Ben was a crack notcher, a notcher being a man who, with a sharp ax, went up to a tree to be sawn down and chopped into it a notch, the position of the notch determining the precise direction in which the tree would fall when sawn from the opposite side of the tree. In our camp it was also the job of the notcher to lop off branches that might be in the way of the sawyers in cutting the tree into logs.

Word had reached the men in camp that Ben in some of his off periods had been a kind of lay preacher. Upon receiving this disquieting news, the rest of the men questioned, I think for the first time, the generally good judgment of Father. They adopted a wait-and-let's-see attitude, however: All they asked was that Ben should not try to mix up his preaching business with his career in camp.

For his part, Ben for a time acquitted himself with a good deal of success. The men observed that while he did not contribute to the meatier of the bull sessions, the point of a good story was not lost on him. He could laugh with the best of them and, what was more important, in the right places. His devotions, if any, were performed in retreats far removed from the shanty, and that helped.

Then came a day when the urge to do things for people got the better of Ben and he ventured one Sunday to services in the Gibbs school. Before he returned to camp he had made arrangements to deliver Sunday sermons during the remainder of the camp season.

Father, when Ben gave him the news, was not too cooperative: Ben, the dinged so and so, could go down to the Gibbses and preach his head off, but he'd be a blankety-blank so-and-so if he'd let him have a horse for the trip down.

Sky Pilots brought religion into the lumber woods, often making long trips through rough, stormy weather in severe cold.

COURTESY OF DOROTHY PAYTON

So it was that Ben set out afoot for the Gibbs school. An hour later the entire camp, except Old Pat and George Kent, who was nursing a cold, set out for the same destination on a set of bobs that Father urged them to use.

Ben was announcing his text when our camp strode in, boisterously, taking seats wherever vacant ones could be found. Summoning their best manners, they listened attentively to the sermon; a few joined in the singing of the closing hymn, and all listened with decorum to the benediction. Then, while the sky pilot was receiving appreciative sentiments from the regular communicants, the jacks strode out to the sleighs and, sleigh bells jingling, were on their way back to camp.

An hour and more later, Ben came into camp, and in a surly mood. Since this did not soften during the day, the men decided to put him up. This form of punishment was a means whereby an unbroken spirit was hailed before the camp's "judge," evidence heard, and sentence pronounced by Judge Hank Leary.

In announcing his decision, Leary enlarged upon the recalcitrance of the spirit displayed by the culprit, reviewed the evidence presented, dwelt upon the peavey as a superior tool in handling burling logs, touched upon lugheads like left-handed sawyers, and sentenced the convicted culprit to being put up, and immediately. The Judge ordered the Head Blanket Spreader to lay out a blanket upon the floor of the shanty and the prisoner to stretch out upon it. He called upon the six Raisers of the Blanket to do their stuff, and the High Executioner, Mike Higby, to lay to with George Kent's bootjack.

Mike applied the bootjack to Ben's posterior with the greatest enthusiasm until Ben's resistance was broken down; he acknowledged his errors and quickly was laid upon a bunk to nurse the jolt to his pride. No further mention of the affair was made by any of the men, but within a week Ben had left camp and, by the family at least, was never heard of again.

The incident marked the only time in the history of our camp when a man was "put up" except in good fun and when a jack had laughingly pleaded guilty to an accusation made in the same spirit. I recall that Emory Lewis, one year when he was Judge, imposed sentence upon himself for some ludicrous offense, receiving an even dozen smart whacks bestowed in good fun.

John the Pole, as everybody knew him, was with us this same winter, in those few months demonstrating a knack that bordered on genius with white birch bark. With a sharp penknife and a heavier knife, along with strips of the bark and thin slices of dried white pine, he fashioned wondrous snuffboxes. With the greatest skill he shaped the edges of the strips, of varying widths, into points and curlicues, and with equal skill he cut the pine into faultless oval shapes of extreme thinness. A half dozen of the bark strips were laid one upon another, each narrower than the one beneath it. These were bent around the two ovals, one at either side, and fixed in place with tiny wooden pegs reaching through into the pine ovals. The completed case, lacquered and lightly stained, was beautiful in the extreme, pleasing all to whom John gave them, which meant every man in camp and the ladies of the household.

It was John who dubbed me the "little smeller feller." The reference was to the fact that in the woods, in any season, I was always going about and trying out the odors of flowers, of plants and trees and the like and identifying them, in a tentative kind of way.

John was the most talented of all our camp men and I was overcome when I learned that he would not return the following season.

It was another winter that we had in camp a Frenchman from Quebec, as restrained in speech as John was voluble. Louie did things as quaint as John with the language, and like John was handy with a pocketknife. I was already outgrowing elm roots as a medium of smoking, and with the greatest delight was flirting with tobacco. No secrecy was involved. When I pulled at a root or a corncob, it was often with Mother looking on, though with no great degree of enthusiasm. She made no comment, and smoking before her seemed to me sweeter than smoking down behind the barn would have been.

I was already outgrowing elm roots as a medium of smoking, and with the greatest delight was flirting with tobacco. No secrecy was involved. When I pulled at a root or a corncob, it was often with Mother looking on, though with no great degree of enthusiasm. She made no comment, and smoking before her seemed to me sweeter than smoking down behind the barn would have been.

Louie found no fault with my evil habit, yet was outraged by the corncob. Coming across a seasoned elm burl, he sawed out a small square, pipe size, and with a brace and bit made a hole for the bowl and with the end of a poker burned a hole for the stem. A little sandpapering, and the beauteous pipe was mine. Louie seemed pleased when I murmured my equivalent of thanks and gave me enough tobacco to fill up. The two of us sat on a bench and sealed our very special friendship in a pall of impenetrable smoke.

Even with so glorious a pipe, however, I had not achieved the ultimate in smoking elegance. The following winter one of our men, Ed Brooks, was doubly addicted to the weed: He smoked and chewed at one and the same time. I accepted the fact as a challenge and in no time at all I was forever following in Ed's footsteps.

If I was errant throughout my early nicotine routines, the fault possibly could be traced to Father's appointment of Fred as keeper of the stores. The stores referred to such items as we kept in stock for the men—several kinds of smoking and chewing tobacco, snuff, needles and thread, socks, mittens and such.

Fred made notations of the various charges in a tall, yellow-paged account book. For his assistant I selected myself, and in that capacity I dedicated my efforts to the vast supply of tobacco in every form. Acorn, Jolly Tar, Snuff—I loved the smell of each brand, sniffing loudly as I tried out the odor of this kind of tobacco and that and begging the tobacco tags when the men came in for chewing. The stamps I attached to hat or cap, as the season might be, setting myself up, if not as the best-dressed man in camp, yet certainly the most glittering one whenever the sunlight caught the shining shades of my headgear.

Chapter Fifteen

Suckers Get a Break

© R.P. Nadeau

LIFE IN A
NORTH WOODS
LUMBER CAMP

OLD PAT might be supreme authority in the sport of sitting on a bank and waiting for a shiner to come along and nudge an undersized worm. Spearing at night for suckers with a jack at the back end of your raft, was something better. This latter science was Fred's and my very special province. It was a man's business! You might scorn the hole-to-hole kind of fishing, but here in spearing was action: you went out with your pike pole and got 'em!

Four of us made up a spearing expedition that set forth late one April evening. Nobody in the outfit had a set of rules to go by but we were in possession of a few general principles, notably the facts that the business was done at night, that the blacker the night the better, that lacking a boat you could use a raft, that at the back end of the craft must be a jack light filled with flaming pine knots, and that the crew must be made up of at least two hands: one armed with a pike pole for getting the raft up- or downstream and the other to stand ready with poised spear to strike down such suckers as were foolish enough to get on the beam. With these ideas to guide us, we could be counted upon to improvise should need arise.

Father was right when he said that the occasion called to high heaven for a boat. Boats, however, were unknown in Greendale. It was a year or two later that in St. Louis I saw my first boat, and a look at the contrivance convinced me that all this talk about boats was just come-on stuff put out by people who sold the cussed things. It never occurred to me that in Detroit, to cross the wide river into Canada, you didn't just go down to the shore and with a peavey hop onto a log that somebody had left there. When I did learn the facts about boats, the business of living lost for me much of its charm. I moped about the house for days, until Mother threatened to give me a cold pack, the only sure cure for attacks of shaking ague that caught up with me each autumn.

A raft, such as we used on our sucker safaris, was a simple contrivance made by lining up, side by side, three or four logs of approximately the same length and binding them together by cross pieces held firmly in place by spikes that could be sunk deep into the log. (In Greendale a spike was any nail longer than those of the ten-penny class.) Such was the weight of the craft that it would require a good deal of tugging and hauling to get it into water in which it could float. Eventually you were free and, bound up- or down-stream, singing, like as not, the first verse of "Suwanee River," which was all of the song that you knew.

To go downstream was a matter merely of keeping the craft in the current, the instrument for the purpose being a pike pole, or, if you preferred, a peavey, the latter the log driver's favorite instrument. The pike pole did not serve so many purposes as the peavey, being merely a long pole turned from dried and seasoned hard timber, preferably hickory. At the business end, an iron spike was driven in, the pole reinforced at the spot by an iron band to prevent splitting. The riverman, by jabbing the pike into a log, could draw it to him, or himself to a log. With it, too, the driver would be adept at keeping his balance while riding a fractious log.

For spearing operations this night of nights a basket, fabricated by Fred, with my incomparable help, from iron barrel hoops, was rigged to the stern of the raft. In it was put an assortment of pitchy pine knots to be set afire. The theory, and usual practice, was that the silly suckers, being just that for the light, would crowd around the raft and practically ask for a three-tined spear to be lambed into their midribs.

This dark night, then, we set out upon our voyage. The crew consisted of Father, who, the strong man of the outfit, took number one position. This, as Fred had worked it out, was as navigator and pike pole manipulator; Fred, who manned the spear; I as supercargo but also carrying a spear, a small one that our blacksmith had turned out for me; and Old Pat, also supercargo, with number one rating, as befitting a veteran with so long and illustrious a military career.

The raft had been put together on Potter Creek. There it was boarded one night after supper and eased down over treacherous shoals to the Salt, a hundred yards below.

Upon arrival at the Salt, golden minutes were lost in trying to decide whether we should go upstream or down. The upstream adherents, made up of Fred and me, won when Fred advanced the argument that since the fish would be headed upstream the best way to get them would be to sneak up on them from behind. The same argument would have worked the other way around, but this involved a type of thinking beyond our simple techniques.

So it was that we set out under darkling skies. Going upstream, you would keep out of the current if you knew what was good for you. In any case, it made no difference with the suckers. Whether they were lying in the current or in some place thinking up new ways of being foolish, they would, upon seeing the light, dash over to find the most likely location for being impaled upon the tines of a spear.

Poling a raft could be achieved by standing at the back end, jabbing the pike into the bottom of the river, leaning against it and pushing, or standing in the front end and pushing, as the craft moved, shoving for all one was worth and walking along the side to the stern. And so on all over again, and again, until the outfit had reached the objective of the expedition, if by some miracle the poler lasted that long.

The presence of the flare, just beneath which the suckers were supposed to congregate in expectant mood, complicated the business, and so tonight the navigator stood in one spot at the front and just pushed.

Father's was an extraordinary performance, and we made better than fair progress. After a half hour or so, Fred spied a long, black form following just back of the raft and in the outer circles of the light. In his excitement, he turned to mention it to Father, only to catch the navigator in the shin with the spear. Father, caught completely off guard, cried, "By the jumping Jeeeehoshaphat and all the little Jeeeehoshaphats," an expression of his usually reserved for ceremonial occasions. Turning aside to avoid another flourish of the spear, he slipped and fell overboard in three feet of water.

Father, caught completely off guard, cried, "By the jumping Jeeeehoshaphat and all the little Jeehoshaphats," an expression of his usually reserved for ceremonial occasions. Turning aside to avoid another flourish of the spear, he slipped and fell overboard in three feet of water.

Meantime I had been up and about and in the general excitement caught Old Pat in the midriff with my own spear. The old soldier, erstwhile toast of generals and colonels, who was standing on the outside log, swung out neatly and clipped Fred on the ear, a performance that was rewarded with howls.

When Father had been brought aboard, Fred murmured that he was sorry, a sentiment received by Father with a smile, and presently we were underway again. We had gone two or three bends and as many straightaways when Pat shouted "Fish!" with the same nonchalance as in the war he had received the General's encomiums. Fred had seen them at the same time—three huge lunks lying along the bottom tandem fashion. Fred heaved the spear and hauled in one of the trio, a squirming creature that tested Fred's strength and sang-froid before it was landed in the bushel basket that in supreme optimism we had brought along.

Father told Fred that it was a fancy job and started poling again. Up around where Spring Brook entered the river, Fred caught sight of a group of fish that followed the raft, only to be blacked out one minute and then being again in what they seemed to consider their favorite spot. Something eerie seemed to be afoot when suddenly they remained in sight long enough for Fred to hurl his spear. This gave him his second trophy.

While Father was bestowing encomiums upon Fred's prowess, we drifted onto a sandbar and here we remained for a few minutes for the excitement to disappear. We made use of it to discuss the disappearing and reappearing fish that had caught Fred off balance. Father worked it out that trees momentarily threw shadows across the stream, which shows that a little worry about trees is sufficient.

Pat, no doubt, was thinking of the battle at Cold Spring when, startled as our prizes began lunging right and left in the basket, I slid off the raft into water almost to my chin, noiselessly and unmissed by the rest of the crew. Father at last looked around.

"Where's the kid?"

Nobody answered, and I had a feeling of nobody caring very much. I knew, however, that at great historical moments the true fisherman keeps his dam trap shut, wherefore I stood silent in the dark waters. All poling ceased, and the three crewmen peered this way and that, only, their vision affected by the flare, to peer in vain. Father moved the raft to one side lest, I supposed, I might be underneath. I wasn't, and they decided to drift downstream. They could at least look for the body!

It was now Pat's turn to be clipped by Fred's spear. He caught the upper end of the shaft across an ear, and in his surprise stepped too far to the left and went overboard. He was promptly rescued, but not before the raft had drifted yards below me. I now decided that my only chance for succor lay in making my whereabouts known. I would do it in the best traditions of the Greendale forest, and so let go with our old "Ho-lo, ho-lo-lo" cry.

"Cleanup crews" worked in boats and from shore as a sort of "rear guard" to make sure that every last log reached its destination at the mill. These men combed the banks, freed minor log jams, and got all of the timber that might have been delayed in its downstream journey moving again.

COURTESY OF LAWTON L. WILLIAMS

"What's that?" I heard Father ask. "It sounds like an owl."

Fred encouraged him in the idea and, since they were getting farther and farther from me, I decided upon drastic measures and let loose with my favorite expletive, supposed never to be uttered in the presence of Father or Mother.

"Damn!"

"Owl my foot," said Father. "It's the kid."

They poled back upstream for me, and once I was aboard the lugger, all tensions I could see were eased when Father said why not call it a day. The motion was carried.

The sucker had a cousin, the redhorse. The two fish, so far as I could see, were alike in all respects except size. Each had large, silvery scales, the same red fins and tails, and identical puckering-string mouth. The redhorse grew, however, to a size of six to eight pounds, double the size of the sucker. In taste appeal, the redhorse was one up on the sucker, there being so much more of him. At the time, what with our uncultivated tastes, they were the last word in desirability.

The family had heard about a kind of red-horse tournament, or festival, indulged in each spring at the Halfway Dam on the Chippewa River. Annually when the redhorse were running people came into the woods from as far away as Shepherd and Mount Pleasant—farmers and villagers, whole families of them. They brought barrels and salt for preserving the catch against the winter months to come. They came with tents and brought cases filled with foodstuffs and cooking utensils, since they would be staying for days.

Tournaments of the Red Horse

© R.P. Nadeau

LIFE IN A
NORTH WOODS
LUMBER CAMP

The dam owed its name to the fact that it lay approximately halfway between Midland to the east and Mount Pleasant to the west. Above the dam a few rods, the road from Midland sent a branch southwestward, to pass our camp on its way to Shepherd.

In every direction the dam was shut in by a wondrous growth of pine, which in the warm days of spring filled the nostrils with the sweet smell of pitch. All this, with the blue in the sky and the silvery ribbon of river as the Chippewa plunged over the spillway and disappeared in the forest, was too much for a little fellow's senses, and he would be glad when Bat Masheau, who tended the dam, came across the river to see Father and said how fast you were growing and you'd be a man yet before your mother was.

Bat and his wife, with their two sons, lived just at the other end of the dam, in a house sided with upright pine boards, weather-stained now to a shade that blended with the forest around it. He was short and on the pudgy side, fascinating me beyond measure by reason of the single gallus, over his left shoulder, which held up his faded overalls, the legs of the latter rolled halfway to the knees over the tops of high, tightly-laced river shoes. I never discovered what became of the other gallus, a mystery that disturbed me for many years. Fred, when one time I was brooding upon the mystery, asked why I didn't ask old Bat and get it over with. The answer could have been that in Bat's presence I was always too frightened to talk.

Father had told me that Bat was part Indian and part French. That, I felt, was bad enough, but when I found that this made him a half-breed, my fear of the man went beyond all bounds. He might speak to me, and ever so gently, but my only reply would be a series of nods and other spectacular motions of the head.

Bat and Father seemed to be great friends, and yet I was always surprised when Father emerged from the house without a knife dangling from his back, or at least with a black eye as a souvenir of the occasion.

At such times as they opened the dam, Jake and Ed to my mind were more evil of aspect, if that be possible, than their father. Starting at either end of the dam, the young men pulled up the heavy upright timbers that held back the water. These they laid side by side upon heavy sleepers stretching across the dam. In this manner they made a sound and solid floor beneath which the released water swept and swirled in its impatience to be free.

Here, under cover of Father's protective presence, although an eye was always out for Bat, I would spend hours, looking through spaces between the timbers at the rushing water beneath, peering over the edge at the clouds of spray rising above the spillway, and shying stones at bits of debris floating toward the dam.

Such was the Halfway Dam, and when Father remarked to Fred what say we drive down tomorrow and look the redhorse business over, my own enthusiasm was thrown into high gear. Just the three of us would make the trip, Father said, Old Pat to be left behind to guard the women folks. We wouldn't stay overnight. Just go down and look around.

Next morning we hitched Powder Face to the buggy and the three of us set out. A couple hours and we were there, and Fred and I agreed that the sight that met our eyes more than lived up to advance notices.

Below the dam the shores were lined with large square dipnets, rigged for raising and lowering by means of long poles mounting long sweeps. It was an awesome sight, what with the roar of the water pouring over the dam, the back water eddying in white, rushing waves deep along the banks. Everywhere among the trees, wagons were parked, horses tied to wagon wheels and nibbling at armfuls of hay placed on the ground at their feet. Women were busy with barrels, packing redhorse in them; a dozen or more children, mostly in the way, were cluttering up the scene, while at the nets the menfolks, according to the ladies, were having all the fun.

After observing the scene for a time, one could not be convinced that the men were not on the short end of the holiday. Every so often at a given net two or three men would throw their weight upon the shore end of the sweep, bringing the net out of the water, jerking and with a swishing sound, and causing the catch of fish to be jounced up and down. When the sweep had been swung in a way to bring the net close to shore, one of the men armed with a net attached to a long pole gathered in the catch, fish by fish.

Fred and I, having solved the secret of the various techniques used in netting, soon were pondering upon what to do next. This was a serious problem, with so many things going on, and so many things not going on that somebody ought to get something started. Fred observed that the over-all sight was better than Barnum's Circus, and I ventured that it was a hell of a lot better.

Father had walked across the dam and was talking with old Bat, and as a concession to my misgivings of old Bat Fred remarked what say we tackle the long rafts of square oak timbers assembled well below the spillway and destined for ship-building yards at Bay City.

It was grand fun running up and down the long timbers and imagining we were pacing the deck of a noble ship, even if we didn't have a wooden leg between us, a patch over the eye and a pirate flag floating from an imaginary mast.

This went on until past lunchtime, when Father came up and said how about eating.

"I'll bring it!" And Fred was off with a bound toward the buggy over among the trees.

"Wait," Father called after him. "The Masheaus want us to eat with them."

"In the house?" I asked, and when Father said "Yes," I shuddered and told him I was going to eat my part of the lunch with Powder Face. I persisted in spite of Father's glowing description of the hot biscuits and wild honey we were to have. One of the Masheau boys last summer had cut a bee tree, and Father smacked his lips. I was counting on Fred's agreement with me, but the prospect of warm biscuits and honey lured him away.

The upshot of the new turn of events was that I ate lunch alone, and under the approving eye of Powder Face, expecting any moment to see Father dash from the Masheau dungeon bearing the mangled form of my brother. I found consolation in the fact that I need not go hungry, and when I had emptied my lunch pail I started in on Fred's, and had practically made my way through to his pie when I suddenly stretched out on the lap robe and fell asleep.

> ...we were suddenly aware of an excited crowd gathering at the foot of the dam. Somebody had raised a record catch and the net was filled with a mass of squirming, gleaming fish.

The afternoon was half over when Fred shook me and said come on, let's run races on the dam. As a game to rouse the sporting instinct, racing across a dam proved to be no great shakes. Although Fred imposed a considerable handicap upon himself so that I could beat him by a neck, even if you got there first what did you have?

We were both thinking about going down and giving the two kids from Mount Pleasant a going-over when we were suddenly aware of an excited crowd gathered at the foot of the dam. Somebody had raised a record catch and the net was filled with a mass of squirming, gleaming fish.

In his hurry to get to the scene, Fred decided to take a short-cut and when we reached the end of the planking he cut down the steep bank instead of continuing along the causeway and coming in from behind the nets. Had his plan not gone afoul, he would have saved perhaps a minute in time and a few steps. Half the distance between the dam and the netful of fish, a foot slipped and Fred was plunged into the eddying backwater. For his age he was a good swimmer, but there was danger of his being swept under the dam. Men shouted and ran along the bank. Father, dashing across the dam, was about to jump in to the rescue when suddenly the number one net was raised, with Fred and a half dozen redhorse in it.

Fred had no sooner been carried to the bank than I burst into howls and Father, after thanking the rescuers, hitched Powder Face to the buggy and we were on our way home.

For a long time nobody spoke, Fred from shivering in his wet clothes and I because I was not familiar with the sentiments appropriate to the occasion that had been so nearly dire. It was understood, I think, that the incident would remain a secret with us men, and even by us forgotten as soon as possible. No use worrying Mother, who didn't have too high a regard anyhow for Father's capacity to oversee two young boys. The implied pact was lived up to, except that whenever Father wanted to tease Fred he might say, with an ill-suppressed smile, "Well, old redhorse, how about it?" This only if we three were present. With Mother present Father's routine might be, "Well, old horse, what do you say, eh?"

ONE MORNING, soon after the drive, I heard the devastating news that the schools at Cedar Lake and in the Gibbs neighborhood were not the only institutions of learning in the world. I was informed that Shepherd had one, and Midland—any number of places apparently had them. The information came at breakfast when Mother informed Father that it was high time that Tom got some schooling. And after him the two girls would be coming along.

Chapter Seventeen

Little Log Schoolhouse

© R.P. Nadeau

LIFE IN A NORTH WOODS LUMBER CAMP

It was a lot of nonsense. My convalescence I always spent looking at pictures in copies of the *Midland Sun*, a fascinating journal with which the walls of my room were papered. I could pick out "cat" and "dog" with the best of them. More than that, Mother was teaching me the entire alphabet and I could, with a terrific scrawl, make a go at writing my name. School indeed!

Breakfast over, I got Fred into a huddle down back of the barn. From him I learned the sad truth. Schools were everywhere. And you had to go to them whether you wanted to or not. He reassured me on only one point: a school brought together a flock of kids that made fighting practically a continuous activity.

"Take here," Fred told me. "If you want to give Jones what's coming to him you have to go up to his house, and the same with the Hart kid. What a school does is bring them all into one place and any time you want to lambaste somebody all you have to do is just go up and let him have it."

That seemed a satisfactory if not a particularly glowing reason for having schools, wherefore I accepted them as something you had to attend or you hadn't, and I viewed with no ardor the feverish efforts that were soon under way to get a school going, right here in our very midst. Father, as Mother was wont to put it, was not one to let grass grow under his feet.

First, of course, must come the setting up of a school district, and a trip by Father to Midland soon brought official papers, which called for the election of three Directors. Father, Alex Jones and Ben Hodgins were chosen, with Father as Chief Director. A term of three months was decided upon, a start as soon as arrangements could be made.

The only problem that seemed to worry Father was finding a teacher. He told Mother that this would mean a lot of letter-writing and didn't she think we ought to have some adequate and official stationery? Mother did, and Father thereupon decided to drive to Shepherd next morning. There he knew a printer who could fix him up.

Before setting out, Father reminded himself that the right front tire on the buggy was loose and he would have to go down to the stable and give it a good soaking. I informed him that I would help with the tire if he would let me go to town with him. To this, after a good deal of haggling, customary on such occasions, he agreed, with the greatest solemnity, his final stipulation being that he would let me go with him provided that I on my part did not help him. He relented, however, to the extent of saying I could look on. I promised to stay ten feet from any and all operations, which he knew meant that I would be on top of and all over him.

Father also knew that I might also have my uses. Helping Father in almost anything that involved tools meant much fetching and carrying.

The weather had turned hot and dry, and tire trouble was chronic, the heat not only expanding the tires but also shrinking the "fellies." Loose tires had to be soaked in water, for which purpose we possessed something startling: a patented steel tire trough, in which, filled with water, the wheel when jacked up could be turned and the felly soaked evenly all the way around.

Father backed the buggy out of the shed and then couldn't find the trough. I recalled where I had been using it down on Black Creek as an experiment station in my tadpole research—Fred had told me that tadpoles would turn into five-legged frogs if you put them in water with plenty of salt in it. I would fetch the trough for Father, and did, first ascertaining that in all the hours since early morning nothing had happened and then putting the pollywogs in the creek.

All was at last in place and Father turned the wheel slowly, and so expertly that I asked if I couldn't do it. With a show of great reluctance he turned the job over to me, and I was still twirling the wheel an hour later when Fred came to see why I hadn't answered the supper bell.

Next morning after breakfast we were off. Scarcely during the eight miles to Shepherd were my eyes off the tire, so gratifying was its perfect performance. Out some five or six miles, near the Roberts farm, we had to cross the Big Salt in its upper reaches. Instead of using the bridge, however, Father drove through the river alongside the bridge, a proceeding that had the two-fold advantage of letting Powder Face reach his head down and take on a supply of water and wetting the tires—not that any of the tires displayed signs of dropping off, but on general principles. You always did that in summer when you came to a stream.

It was great fun riding places with Father. Summers, if you drove along the woods road to Midland, you drank in the sweet smells that came off the evergreens, and from the underbrush and berry bushes that grew up close to the wagon tracks, the road so narrow that in long stretches a sharp click-click-clickety-click of projecting low growths was heard as the spokes of the wheels brushed against them.

Along the roads outside, such as those going to Shepherd or Mount Pleasant, you could see for miles across well-tilled fields, bobolinks hovering above the meadows and giving you a taste of song that you didn't get in the woods and a pungent smell of tansy and wild geranium that grew in profusion close up to the wheel tracks.

In Greendale you rode over long stretches of sand and were fascinated as you followed the wheel beside you as it rolled over and over through the white, powder-like sand. As you watched you saw the sand close over the felly and, riding up a space, drop in a filmy, yellow curtain draping both sides of the wheel.

On these sandy reaches, too, you might see a great cloud of dust loom up, far down the road, and you would wonder who was in the middle of it. It might be Old Man Gibbs, and he would be wondering the same thing about the cloud that you were kicking up.

Along here at some point you might come to a place where the road widened sufficiently to permit two rigs to pass each other, and you would turn out to wait for the other rig to come along and pass you.

Whoever it was would presently arrive and stop, and the two of you would be talking about how the country was going to the dogs, the way the old mossbacks in Washington were running things, and although half an hour passed, as you drove on, dust would still be settling from the cloud stirred up by Old Man Gibbs when first approaching you.

Father had his own way of riding in a buggy. For miles he would lean forward, his arms bent and resting along his legs, his brown derby on the back of his head and over near one ear, and his eyes in the general direction of the whipsocket. Then after a half hour or so he would straighten up, put his hat low over one eye and drop his right leg dangling outside the box or resting on the step. All the while he would be humming some well-known hymn, more often than not "Beulah Land." What it was that he pondered during those long sessions with himself I never asked: I was smart enough to keep my dam trap shet.

Driving with Father in winter was something else completely. He was jovial then, always humming the airs of old Irish ballads—when, that is, he was not bantering me. Maybe he was merely reflecting the moods of Powder Face, who, the cutter gliding noiselessly behind him, fairly flew over the white miles.

In any event, the visit to the printer in Shepherd yielded a dozen pads of letterheads, with Father's name glorious in big Gothic letters across the top of each sheet and something about School District Number 2, and a line on which the date could be put down. And, as if this were not enough, Father had secured envelopes to match!

"Anybody getting a letter on stationery like that would want to come and teach without pay," said Mother, smiling when she saw it.

Writing lessons in the little log schoolhouse might have sparked Tom O'Donnell's calling to write professionally. A few short years before his death, he satisfied a lifelong yearning to tell the many stories about the Chippewa, Big and Little Salt rivers, the Michigan forests through which they flow, the mills and industries which were founded upon their banks, and the men whose foresight and genius started those enterprises.

COURTESY OF PAT PAYNE

I doubt whether the paper and envelopes were that good, yet one of the responses brought a reply from Sadie Cook, who didn't wait for a reply but drove in, a day or two later, from her home over beyond Mount Pleasant. Sadie gave Father to understand that for the thirty dollars a month and board that was offered he might just as well close the deal then and there. The transaction was quickly consummated.

This achieved, Sadie asked, "Where is the school-house?"

"Huh!"

It had never occurred to Father that here was a detail to be settled, and with school to open in two weeks! As though it had been settled long ago, however, Father pointed to the men's shanty across the road.

"We'll take the bunks out for the summer. The term will be over and the bunks put back before the men come into camp in the fall. After all, it is only for three months."

Sadie was shaken. "Only three months? In the whole year?"

Sadie's glance took me in as if to say that a kid like that could stand, at the very least, twelve months. Father, however, informed Sadie that we'd start off with three months and maybe next summer we could work five in.

The next two weeks were given over to feverish preparations for the opening of school, with carpenters brought in from Shepherd. Bunks were removed from the shanty and the necessary furniture fabricated, seats for the children to be made from long pine boards planed to a smooth, satiny finish.

> What Paul Revere was to the approaching hostilities at Lexington, not to mention Concord, we were to the opening of school in District Number Two. Sadie's buggy had scarcely rattled over the loose planking of the Potter Creek bridge than Fred and I dashed out of the house to spread the tidings.

The results of so much labor were exciting. Along either side of the shanty ran a bench, and in front of it, supported by upright pieces, was a wide board, on a tilt to serve as a desk. Underneath was a narrower board on which we could keep our books when not immediately in use, ink, pens, pencils, slates and slate pencils and slate rags. One bench was dedicated to the girls, and across the room facing them was a duplicate arrangement for the boys. The wide space between the two benches was a kind of neutral territory.

No regulations covered the manner of getting to the particular place on the long bench, which was yours, be it at or near the end, or in the middle, a half dozen feet from the end. It seemed to be within the rules, if you were a boy, to go up to the spot and step over the bench. The more brazen of the girls used the same technique, and there were occasions when the tinier of them went to their respective places and crawled under.

Fred and Will Jones used whatever method would attract most attention at the time. Their favorite way was to come in, just before the bell rang, from the front end, squeezing in between the seat and the desk in front. This compelled everybody to rise, and the trick was to see how many sets of toes could be stepped on. Eight out of ten was par for the course.

A blackboard ran across the end of the room back of the teacher's table, the table something that Father had used as a desk and now was loaning to the District. Along the blackboard ran a projecting strip for holding the sticks of chalk, while at one end, on a nail driven into a log, hung a cloth for making erasures.

Entrance to the shanty was by a door at the end opposite the teacher's desk. In either wall, the long way of the shanty, were two small windows of four panes each.

All this was at Father's expense; even the school bell was supplied from our camp—the handbell used for bringing the men to the house at mealtime. The only cost to the District was what Sadie, in her lighter moments, referred to as her "income."

Thus were the preparations for the opening of school completed. There remained only the business of spreading word of this startling event. This detail Fred and I took on our own shoulders, and right well we carried on. What Paul Revere was to the approaching hostilities at Lexington, not to mention Concord, we were to the opening of school in District Number Two. Sadie's buggy had scarcely rattled over the loose planking of the Potter Creek bridge than Fred and I dashed out of the house to spread the tidings. By supper time, so efficient had been our efforts, the story had been proclaimed to one and all, even to regions as remote as those of the Parsonses and Harts, that at nine o'clock, tomorrow morning, school would convene in District Number Two.

Reception of the tidings was much the same everywhere. The response of Mrs. Hodgins, while pleasing to Fred and me, would have been more gratifying had it been more universal:

"Land sakes, boys, you look hot and tired. Come on in and let me give you something to eat!"

And Bud's "Give me a piece too, Ma," equally indicated the attitude of the victims of the impending tragedy.

HAD SADIE, full of energy and good sense, been a less practical little body she would have looked over the boys assembling that first morning at school and, violently disturbed, hurried tothe house for her things and dashed for home. Each of the nine came in blue overalls: not the kind with bibs, as in latter years could be seen in nostalgic school-day shows, but just plain overalls, held up by more or less grimy suspenders.

Depending upon the length of service they had seen and the frequency with which they had been scrubbed, the overalls ran the entire gamut of shades, from the deep blue of the newly "boughten" ones to the pale azure of those that had seen long service. Patches were all over them at strategic places, and here and there could be seen a patch upon a patch, and with the thread beginning to show thin.

The newish overalls would be rolled halfway to the knees, but these were overshadowed, in point of number, by the "high-water" ones, which long ago, from periodical washings, had started crawling up the legs. Pants at this stage would be, more often than not,

Chapter Eighteen

My After-School Agenda

© R.P. Nadeau

LIFE IN A
NORTH WOODS
LUMBER CAMP

a perfect form fit, and if a boy was heavy set, like Will Jones, you were aware of little else except blue bulges, considerably in evidence from where the teacher sat, and you feared the worst should Sadie take it into her head to lay Will across her knee for a well-deserved walloping.

Every kid of course held his pants in place with galluses, which had been fashioned with an eye to their proper functioning. In most cases they were from an inch to two inches wide and were attached to buttons, or when a button famine was on the attachment was to wooden pegs run through openings in the band cut by a knife.

If you wanted to be perfectly de rigeur, and you did, you decorated your galluses all over with tin tobacco tags, with an eye to the greatest possible variety. You couldn't avoid having a lot of the Jolly Tars, the little red tags. Nearly everybody, it seemed, smoked and chewed Jolly Tar, wherefore without some smart trading you would be swamped with the tags.

If you were a good trader there would be no reason why you had not accumulated specimens even of the beautiful Acorn stamp, and tags shaped like letters of the alphabet, and tags in geometrical patterns.

John Wilsey had the largest collection of tobacco tags. So gloriously were John's galluses decorated with stamps, of every color and shape, that when you saw him coming down the road, the sun catching him, you thought of the Black Knight glinting all over the field of Crecy.

In the headgear department, every kid was on his own, except that everybody wore something. If you were a boy, more likely than not you sported in summer a straw number. Such a hat was made gay by a bright-colored band a half inch wide and a wide brim that flapped up and down when you ran. You probably had been out in the rain with it, and this had thrust it up the middle of the crown to a sharp point, an inch or more in height.

Then there were black or blue cloth caps, which you wore with the peak down over one eye, giving you an abandoned look. John Wilsey, whose general demeanor and appearance were of utter depravity anyhow, wore one of his father's black felt hats. It was two or three sizes too large, and his mother had taken it in with thread, while John had covered it as thoroughly as he had his galluses with tobacco tags.

With the girls it was different. All wore straw hats, mostly prim, simple jobs of sailor shape, ends of ribbon draping the rim. Each wore pigtails, tied together at the ends with blue or pink bows, or else hooked up and tied with a ribbon in the general region of the back of the neck. One or two came fancy, with the braid run around the top of the head, thus creating the general effect, I thought, of a tea mat.

In the footwear department, Sadie's next impression must have been of feet. Hardly a shoe or boot marred the effect of feet on our teacher. The only decorative touch was, here and there, a white rag run around a toe that had been stubbed by contact perhaps with a low-lying root protruding just above the ground. We here speak of the male feet, but the effect would be little different along the opposite bench. The girls also went barefoot, the small of them. Most of the larger ones wore shoes that came half way to the knees, with black cotton stockings that never failed to fascinate Fred and Will.

And when you took note of the gingham and calico dresses, of different shades and patterns—but when Sadie had got that far in her inventory the hour of nine would have come. She let Jennie Parsons ring the bell and the apprehensive battalion came filing in, some to places they had already assigned to themselves, the others taking pot luck.

Sadie said we should all come to order and then say the Lord's Prayer. John Wilsey's galluses might out-glint my own, but at this point we were all up. I did know part of the Lord's Prayer and with a little prompting by Mother I could sometimes stagger through the entire routine. There was no great volume in this first collective effort in what was to be a daily opening, but the time was to come when you could hear the roar of it from as far away as Potter Creek.

Next we had a season of singing. Sadie must have anticipated the worst, for on the blackboard that morning she had written the words of "America." That was all right for those who could read, but it left me and a half dozen others of the young fry to our own devices. Sadie, it may be said to her credit, read the first stanza to us, slowly, and then sang it through. And now, everybody!

The effect was startling. Everybody, including myself, had an energetic go at it. Those who could read kept, as the stanza unfolded, within earshot of one another, but the rest of us branched out into airs peculiarly our own. The result was that while each came in under his own power, the finish would be anywhere from one to two or three laps apart, to end on a note of the singer's choosing. Fred, telling about it at supper that night, said that Nora Jones wound up down in the Gibbs neighborhood, Clara Wilsey somewhere over around Old John Bugbee's, and I myself up on the Bungo Road.

Clearly in this department some good stiff work was indicated, and thereafter prayer was followed until nine-thirty by vocal exercises. For this, Father had brought in a supply of copies of the Knapsack, a popular collection of school songs, from Shepherd.

The singing lesson came to an end out of sheer exhaustion on Sadie's part, and next she turned to the detection of any reading talents latent in the school. From an armful of books she had brought from home, Sadie selected readers for various grades of intelligence. With this effort she would sort her charges into classes. She entered upon the task with beautiful optimism until, handing Will Jones a Fifth Reader, she asked him to read the piece about William Tell and the apple.

The story in the first two or three paragraphs was told in short, simple words, and Will started off like a house afire, except, Sadie pointed out, you didn't call the Alps the Alups. Soon Will was over his head in big words, concentrated with such devastating effect that Sadie was practically doing the reading and Will, looking on, obviously proud of himself.

The Fourth Reader likewise got nowhere, and when it was all over only three classes started off—First, Second and Third Readers. I ended my own effort with something of a flourish because I could identify, and spell with a fair degree of success, thanks to pre-induction tuition by Mother, such profound truths as "The dog can run," and questions no less profound in their implications, like "Can the dog run?" With such a background there was but one thing to do: Put me in the First Reader, much as she would have admired sending me home for keeps.

It was time now for the water to be passed, and to True Hodgins fell the honor. Taking the ten-quart pail from its triangular-shaped shelf in the corner and seizing the long-handled dipper from its nail, True made for the boys' bench and was handing a dipperful to Joe Hart when Sadie corrected him.

"Girls first, True!"

A murmur of protest ran along the line of boys. Whoever'd heard of such dam foolishness! Rebellion seemed about to burst into flame, but True said, "Yes, ma'am," and crossed to the girls' side. Instantly, our resentment was transferred from Sadie to True, and a magnificently-whispered "Sissy!" greeted him.

The water pail went the rounds, with everybody having at least one go at it, and True letting a dipperful run down Will Jones's neck for good

Tom O'Donnell grew to be a serious student of local and regional history. His writing shows a profound grasp of historical background and scrupulous attention to detail which befits his subjects, and yet in the best traditions of historical writing, he included in his stories the boisterous goings-on of the people who once lived robustly in America's back country.

COURTESY OF DOROTHY PAYTON

measure. Mary Parsons asked if she could pass the water in the afternoon, and Sadie said yes.

Spelling was quickly disposed of, and recess was called. A whole fifteen minutes devoted to recess! Not much can be achieved in fifteen minutes, but before the bell rang again we had done pretty well. Immediately we were out of the room, we deployed in divers directions. Most of the girls traipsed over to the house to see our new baby, Myrtle, and most of the boys tore down to Potter Creek to see if Fred and I had been joshing them in talking about the lamprey eels. The eels had been Fred's and my most exciting discovery since coming into the woods. Where they had previously been no one seemed to know, but they were here now, hovering above a bed of pebbles over which the creek flowed in quiet riffles, just a few rods below the bridge.

> On the way back to school, True Hodgins stepped on a bumblebee nest and was stung on the bottom of his left foot for his pains.
> Then Joe Hart, prodding a yellow-jacket nest with a stick, and not to be outdone by a Hodgins, caught one of the insects under the eye.

The doubting Thomases among our audience were convinced of the truth of even our most lurid descriptions of the eels. One question was ventured by Joe Hart. How did we know they were lampreys? We referred Joe to Old Pat as our authority, and the old hero, being a Civil War veteran, with a limp and a cane to prove it, was without cavil accepted as due authority.

On the way back to school, True Hodgins stepped on a bumblebee nest and was stung on the bottom of his left foot for his pains.

Then Joe Hart, prodding a yellow-jacket nest with a stick, and not to be outdone by a Hodgins, caught one of the insects under the eye. That's what they get for being so smart about the eels, Fred told them, and serve them right for not taking our word.

Just then came the recess bell, and we started running for it. As we were doing our gasping best, I saw Fred nudge Will Jones and motion him to follow. A minute later Sadie, as the rest of us were dashing through the door, was transfixed in horror to see Fred come floating into the school-room through the window, followed immediately by Will.

The air was suddenly electric, and when Sadie had sufficiently composed herself she gave the two boys a splendid example of what later on, when I had got into the Fifth Reader, I discovered was scorn. She pointed out how their fathers were Directors and officers of the school district and oughtn't they to be good examples to the younger children? After several more minutes, Sadie ended by sending the offenders home to tell of their evil deeds to their parents, and not to return until tomorrow morning.

The remainder of the morning was taken up with more try-outs in geography and civil government, and at noon Sadie announced a recess for the rest of the day: Mr. O'Donnell was going to Shepherd at once for the readers and other books, and come early tomorrow morning, for school would start again at nine o'clock.

Chapter Nineteen

The Trials of Patrick

© R.P. Nadeau

LIFE IN A
NORTH WOODS
LUMBER CAMP

THE COMING of cows, brought in by Father, had placed new responsibilities upon Pat's shoulders, Father wishing on him the functions of chief tender of cows. Pat was the first in the family, Fred told me, to see the necessity, if you are going to have cows, of having pens in which to keep them. As it turned out we had, at Pat's suggestion, two pens, arranged side by side along the driveway that ran from the barnyard to the road.

One of the pens was to be used by the cows the first year, and after transferral of the animals next year to the second pen, the first would be used as a vegetable garden. Since the shift would be made each spring, this system of fertilization of the soil was a distinct advance over the familiar one whereby you had to carry the fertilizer onto the fields on wagons and spread it around with pitchforks.

Moreover, the plan worked, because year after year our garden brought forth onions and carrots and other salad ingredients of a quality to arouse the ungrudging admiration of friends and passers-by. Pat, regarding the garden as a kind of by-product of the herd, made it his personal province. Any time of day he could be seen on his knees pulling weeds, or else with a hoe hilling up the radishes. For Pat was of the hiller school of gardeners. Let a bean so much as send up a tender shoot and his hoe was on the scene to raise dirt up to and around its neck, adding more and more soil as the plucky sprout persisted in its struggle to rise above the handicaps thought up by the lusty veteran.

With some vegetables, Pat mounded the soil with a hoe into little hills before putting his seeds in. Notable was this in the case of melons of all kinds and the enthusiastic and wide-spreading squash. Such a mound would rise above the surrounding ground to a height of four or five inches and be as much as three feet across. From off the mesa, the vines would trickle in various directions in search of likely places in which to deposit their offspring

Pat's morning activities in the strictly dairying department consisted first, after the milking, of letting down the pen bars. This was a signal to the cows that now for the day they were on their own. Since, except for the cow pens, Greendale was innocent of fences, nobody knew in what direction, or how far, the cattle would go in search of forage. Each wore a bell about its neck, but by ten o'clock the herd would be out of hearing, and although the bells were last heard in the direction of the rollway, which was due east, by mid-afternoon the herd might have made a swing to the south and be eating wild blue-joint along the upper reaches of Onion Creek to the west.

Likely as not, the cows sooner or later would come home by themselves, but Father never was certain and Pat made it his early afternoon chore to start off in search of them. With all of Greendale as a grazing ground, it is a wonder that they ever were found. Pat, however, never failed. His plan each day started from the approximate point at which the bells were last heard and, combining nicely logic and intuition, he would choose one of two possible courses: He would go in the direction in which the bells were last heard, or else he would go in directly the opposite direction. The latter plan was almost always followed by Pat, and nearly always it was successful.

Tom volunteered to arise at 4:30 a.m., and was given the honorary title of "bull whacker" when he went to the barn to do stable chores. He helped feed the horses, tied up bundles of hay, and filled bags of grain for the horses' dinner.

COURTESY OF WINFRED MURDOCK

There were days when the cows would be found as far as two or three miles deep in the wilderness. Upon reaching the herd, it would be any man's guess as to which way was home. The problem had a simple solution: Just show yourself before the cows and, in your best Irish brogue, tell them to "coom on now and get the hell out of there, blast your dom hides, out of there, out!"

At that signal, and with Pat standing by and waiting, the cows would go through a daily routine of rounding up in general assembly to look at one another for the purpose of exchanging ideas as to how they could reach home with the greatest possible annoyance to Pat. The session over, the animals would sniff the air and, determined to make a break for it, would set off in sundry directions.

Presently, the direction of home having been established, the herd would reassemble and, arranging themselves single file behind Bess, a Jersey, they would set out, Pat bringing up the rear. Across swales, through dense growths of osiers in the low places, up such low hills as the landscape afforded and down dales, the cavalcade proceeded.

Now and again a cow, nudged from behind by a sharp horn, would dart off on a tangent of its own. At such moments Pat, limp and all, would start after the miscreant, brandishing his cane and exploding his brogue with an "Out of there, blast your souls, coom out of there, out," until the wayward animal was back in line. An hour, two hours later the cows would be stepping over the lowered bars into the home pen, wearing a look of innocence that would send Pat off to other chores, wondering if the beasts were worthy of his endeavors.

Wintertime, of course, was easy going for Pat. Father had mapped out a feeding schedule, which Pat thought was dom nonsense, but to which he adhered with what for him was a remarkable degree of regularity. Mornings, except on very cold days, cornstalks would be thrown out and the cows released from their stanchions; in the afternoon they would be brought back into the stable for a nap that they had so little earned, according to Pat.

Milking was in the hands of Father and Arnie, the latter also straining the milk and putting it away in crocks. At the milkhouse, at the foot of the hill, was a long row of clean crocks waiting for the milk when it had been put through a fine-mesh wire strainer. That was at first—later on Mother discovered what she considered a more hygienic business: several thicknesses of a fine-mesh cloth, attached by a metal hoop to a bottomless tin through which the milk was poured.

When the water had reached a mean temperature and Father had thrown into it a handful of soft soap brought from the leech, Pat was brought on and informed of the ordeal by water and soap that awaited him. Again he was doomed if he would, but suddenly was aware of the peavey held menacingly in Alex's hand and of an axe helve in Father's.

Once or twice a week, when the sweet, warm milk had been brought in by Arnie, there would be a supper of mush and milk—this would be in spring and summer. Mother always said that you had to be good boys and girls to have this treat provided for you, but since the entire family got in on it we (Fred and I) often discussed the fine points of logic involved, feeling sure that Mother was joking and therefore we need not lay ourselves out too much.

We early discovered that if the herd had one wanton weakness, it was leeks. After the spring drive, and when the high water of the streams had subsided, the first green things to lift their heads above the ground along the flats were wild onions and leeks. The onions grew to the size of overlarge peas and were gathered by us in grand bunches for the evening meal.

Happily the cows never took to the onions, but in a big way they went in for leeks. Nature seemed to inform them of the precise day when the leek season would open. Other times they could take the Potter Creek flats or leave them. Let the first leek appear, however, and the herd would strike out in the morning in a direction due north and in time, having utterly deceived old Pat, would be on the Potter Creek flats. In what for

Pat would be short order, he was down and in their midst. It would be too late and our mush and milk that night would have a flavor that Father always said was worse than garlic and Lord knows, Alice, garlic smells to high heaven. Two or three days later our bread would be spread with butter that was no better.

One morning Pat, determined to steer the cows clear of the ripened leeks, went down to the flats and stood guard all day, only taking time out for dinner. The herd never came near the place, finding, down around Cedar Creek, a mile to the east of our place, another wondrous stand of the toothsome leek he wasn't aware of! Fortunately the leek season lasted but a few days, when the cows would find other ingenious ways of making sure that their milk was on the less-palatable side.

It was at leek time another year that Father, probably thinking about leeks, recalled that Pat had not been turning in his red flannels for the weekly wash. Investigation also disclosed that Pat had been remiss in the detail of his weekly scrub-down in the shanty.

Father immediately confronted the old soldier, and said that a bath impended. Pat said he would be dommed if he'd have a bath, but an hour later, back of the barn, a fire had been started under the huge iron kettle used for making mashes, dosed up with condition powders for both horses and cows. Nearby stood an empty pork barrel, leaning against it what once had been a broom, worn by much use to little more than a stump. Father sent for Alex Jones should Pat exhibit a firm determination to go on being stenchy.

When the water had reached a mean temperature and Father had thrown into it a handful of soft soap brought from the leech, Pat was brought on and informed of the ordeal by water and soap that awaited him. Again he was dommed if he would, but suddenly was aware of the peavey held menacingly in Alex's hands and of an ax helve in Father's. With rare agility, for him, he stripped and climbed into the barrel. Father applied the broom with a vigor that aroused the dander of Pat and the approval of Fred and me, who were observing the bath from around the corner of the barn—and who at supper that night thought how nice Pat smelled.

Chapter Twenty

Berry Picking and My Misery with the Ague

© R.P. Nadeau

LIFE IN A
NORTH WOODS
LUMBER CAMP

IN OUR PART of the lumber woods, blackberries and red raspberries grew in profusion close up to our very doors. Except in uncut timber they were everywhere, preferring to huddle around stumps left by our sawyers.

Having all the berries we could use in our back yard, Father adopted a generous attitude towards visiting pickers as word of our wild fruit treasure got around, at the same time having an eye out for what he regarded as poachers. Father's land and timber holdings covered a considerable region, but all visitors whose general mien was not distasteful to Father were welcome except in an undefined region fairly adjacent to our home, roughly a square mile in extent. Woe betide any pickers that came within this range. Let them so much think of so great an enormity, and Father, doubly armed with a shotgun and Rock, our aging dog, would make a sudden appearance and ask how come.

"Collie" was our favorite description of Rock. The term was vastly misleading, since he could have laid claim to a half-dozen other kinds of blood equal in amounts to the collie content. Everybody agreed that there was a mite of hound in him, but otherwise he aroused in no one the urge to analyze him. He had a vicious mien, growling savagely at the slightest intrusion on his privacy if the whim was upon him, only to soften under the effect of a kind word.

Always on our hunting forays Rock was along, with scarcely a sign that he was aware of his role in the undertaking. With Fred and me he was patient under our weird ministrations, his favorite sport being to dash up and down the river to retrieve bits of wood that, when we had spat on them, we threw into the stream for the purpose.

Such was the right hand, next to a double-barreled shotgun, with which Father confronted astonished poachers on our berry preserves. Fortune favored the family in that intruders, impressed by the armor if not by Father's hostile demeanor, belonged mostly to that persuasion of men who go about shunting wrath this way and that with their soft answers. With such the discussion would start off with ferocity on both sides, a few minutes later to give way to a session of give and take. When this had proceeded for half an hour, Father more often than not would climb into the front seat of the wagon and direct the miscreants to a perfectly dandy patch of berries a half mile away on some ancient logging road.

There were visitors, of course, who regarded the country as a kind of happy berrying ground with communal rights for one and all. These would start off with a show of truculence and ask who was going to stop them. Father, with a look at Rock and the shotgun, would suggest obliquely that this was his particular and very favorite department.

Wintergreen berries grew big in the timber around our schoolhouse. In school our wintergreen berries served a far different purpose than the wondrous wintergreen berry pie Mother baked. When they were in season, boys would come in from recess with pockets bulging with them. Some minutes after the room had become quiet, the girls with their noses deep in their readers, would be clipped behind the ear by a missile snapped by one of the boys from across the room. From another direction other boys in turn would be delivering and retaliating the missiles until the teacher discovered the performance and sent the rogues to stand in the corner for their too-accurate display of marksmanship.

Huckleberries were also to be found, but only in one spot some three miles beyond home on an ancient lumber road, known, by us, as the "Bungo" road. An unfamiliar sojourner might have difficulty in finding the road, but he would be sure of where it should be, for here was a glorious long and curving bank, with the river far below lapping against it.

If the former banking ground did not sufficiently identify the spot, the traveler would be impressed with a considerable area of what once had been cleared land but now was growing up to small undergrowth. This would be, he would say, what had been laid out as a community to be known as Central City. The "central" part of the name would have reference to the fact that the location was, in a very general way, halfway between the cities of Midland and Mount Pleasant. Streets had been laid out, although no sign of their sites remained. Remains of one or two houses could be found, however, and here and there a cedar post to denote, perhaps, the location of a lot.

Father and Mother always planned a yearly camping trip with the Jones family to gather the Bungo huckleberries. There were eight of us, requiring a wagon and a team of horses. Mother and Mrs. Jones made a list of articles to make up the requirements for picking and carrying home the berries, and food for the passengers.

We preferred to leave the wagon and walk, once upon the Bungo road. We found it a more pleasant means of transport, for the entire strip of road was corduroy, laid upon low, swampy ground. The spaces between the upper parts of the logs had once been filled with brush and dirt.

What we were compelled to negotiate were slight remains of soil and brush between the logs, wherefore the wheels of the wagon jounced up and down, up and down, and it was not long before Mother and Mrs. Jones would join us behind the wagon. Fortunately we reached the berry grounds within an hour.

The O'Donnell's saw a growing contingent of rigs of all kinds coming into the settlement, some to spend the day and some with tents for making a two- or three-day stay of berry picking. Tom recalled, "Some of the more ambitious brought jars and other equipment, departing with enough booty to last them through the winter."

COURTESY OF GEORGE SHAUGHNESSY

Setting up camp and a meal were the first order of business. I remember we were satisfied with the old stand-bys: bread and butter overspread with a thick layer of sugar wet down with drops of water and patted down with our fingers. Then came hard-boiled eggs and blackberry pie.

With eating over, each of us was given a pail that either was strung over the neck or swung from the waist or hips—the adults getting a twelve-quart pail. Nora and I were humiliated by each being given a one-quart container with instructions to keep out of the way. Happily, in attempting to honor the instructions, we at once discovered that in the lower places were low, ooze spots with frogs and such. As the afternoon wore on, the elders made worthy accomplishment while the children often became distracted attempting to catch frogs or drifting back to camp to play. This freed the older folks from our constant yammering. Moreover, our position on the sidelines enabled us to check on the worthy accomplishments of our elders. Every half hour or so one of them would come into camp with two pails of berries, and later repeat the performance. For the report, Fred and Will should be credited with but one trip to camp. No questions were raised in the matter, but my own conviction was, as I told in confidence, that they had spent the afternoon playing mumbletty-peg in some quiet, shaded spot.

> The thrill of the camping trip was with the after-supper hour around the campfire. Father would harness a horse and snake into camp a log that seemed dry and calculated to send flames, when lit to the very tops of the surrounding trees...

The thrill of the camping trip was with the after-supper hour around the campfire. Father would harness a horse and snake into camp a log that seemed dry and calculated to send flames, when lit, to the very tops of surrounding trees, the sparks shooting out into space, dead branches snapping as we piled them on, and altogether setting the state for stories and anecdotes.

The womenfolk always sat by themselves on wagon seats placed on the ground. The men swapped experiences gained in lumber camps. Stories might be the drive back in 1875 on the Pine, or the winter when a pack of wolves caught the scaler alone at the rollway and dined on him so thoroughly as to leave little as a souvenir of the occasion except a half acre of blood-stained snow.

During the evening one of the Joneses was bound to ask Father for a song, thus paying tribute to Father's position as host to the party.

Father started out with a ballad that I never remembered all the stanzas to.

As I was a-rambling one morning in May
A beautiful damsel came tripping my way;
Her cheeks were like roses and sweet she did sing,
And she wore a blue handkerchief under her chin.

There were other stanzas but I remember best how it ended.

This couple got married, so I heard people say,
The be-ells did ring and the music did play;
She's no longer a spinner, but wears a gold ring,
And he wears a blue handkerchief under his chin.

There were other songs of a ship blown to bits when its boiler burst. Mother's repertory contained two or three little airs used by her as croons, that I never tired of hearing. One of them, the way she sang it, I still regard as being up there with the Brahms or anybody else's lullaby:

Seven long years since Pompey was dead,
    Yes, yes, Pompey was dead;
The apple tree grew right over his head,
    Yes, yes, over his head.

The apples got ripe and bega-an to fall,
    Yes, yes, bega-an to fall;
There came an old woman to gather them all,
    Yes, yes, gather them all."

And so on through any number of stanzas to the last, which ended, I thought, on a sad and tender note:

> *The saddle and bridle are under the shelf,*
>> *Yes, yes, under the shelf;*
> *If you want any more you can sing it yourself,*
>> *Yes, yes, sing it yourself."*

So was the evening spent, as evenings on trips summer after summer would be spent—singing songs that were old even then. And the morning after would be occupied as this afternoon had been occupied: picking huckleberries and playing.

I remember one summer as I got halfway through my sandwich at lunch that I didn't feel so well. Mother looked at me more and more dubiously and at last cried out, "Tom, you poor child—the ague!" That was it. After a mad scramble to get things, including ourselves, into the wagon and the horse attached, we were on our way, my head in Mother's lap and my mind between shakes wondering how my sister was taking it.

To get the shaking ague you had to come down, on one of the hottest days in summer, with something that you had to be put to bed with, there to shake and shake until the very door knobs rattled. Then you took something bitter that Mother said was quinine. And always there were the cold packs. To take a cold pack you stood up, utterly naked, and let Mother wrap around you a sheet dripping with ice-cold water. Then, with the general effect of Caesar hiking up and down in the forum in the toga that Santa had brought him the previous Christmas, I would be walked over to the bed and covered there with blankets and left to see what would happen.

By that time I wouldn't care. I would wonder if there was any danger of coming apart, like Old Man Adam's buggy did one day, out of sheer cussedness. I shook just from the fever, and now the cold pack started it all over again, only with a quickened tempo and a bright staccato effect. And suddenly would come the realization that the old body was sweating like all get-out.

And a few days later I would be back in school again, holding the young fry spellbound with tales of my ague.

Chapter Twenty-one

Alex Builds a Thresher

© R.P. Nadeau

LIFE IN A
NORTH WOODS
LUMBER CAMP

ALEX JONES, a genius at making useful things, was, the summer of our first Bungo pilgrimage, making a threshing machine. He had cleared some six or eight acres of land, part of which he had put into buckwheat, and it was in anticipation of a good yield that he was looking ahead to the harvest. Power for operating the machine was to be furnished by Will's right arm, who would, as he said, have at least a nice new crank to turn.

As it turned out, Will, as the machine was reaching the completion stages, had spread word of the new thresher to all the boys of the neighborhood. The result of his foresight was that when operations were ready to start Will was standing the kids in line, each awaiting his turn at the crank. Throughout the campaign Greendale breakfasts were hardly completed before the line at the Jones place was forming. At noon there was a dash by every boy for home and a quick dinner, and when this was over there would be the return dash for the Joneses again. Never had so little been achieved by so many.

Alex, a genius at making things with tools,

fascinated Father, who was on the unexpert side in such things. Alex on his part listened ecstatically as Father described to him our home-to-be when the timber was gone. Our home, and the homes that would spring up in the area, would form a community that would thrive, as had the pine trees before it, and would serve as a model for people interested in community-building.

Out of conversations between the two men came a clear conviction that the region was in dire need of a set of scales for the convenience of people having loads of things to be weighed. Father was soon in correspondence with various concerns, and the following spring Alex was putting up a beauteous scale that was shipped to us from Binghamton back in New York State. The location selected for them by Father was almost directly across the road from our house. Keys were kept on a nail on our kitchen; Lew Smith with a load of onions had only to rap at our door for weighing service. Lew had no need of such services, however, as did no one else. Fred and Will tried out a weighing session for the children in the adjacent school, but since their income from the venture was made up mostly of tobacco tags from the boys and the remains of lunches from the girls, the operation was regarded as unremunerative, and the idea was dropped.

The two men were not of the kind to give up. Conversations soon developed around the need in Greendale of a regular threshing machine and steam engine that could be hauled here and there to handle customer harvests of wheat and oats and things. The idea really came out of the success of the machine that Alex was building for threshing his buckwheat.

No sooner said than done, and in the middle of the next summer there arrived in Shepherd complete equipment from a concern that turned out such things in Battle Creek. Father and Alex were ready for this one. Out in Isabella County on selling trips, the two men between Shepherd and Mount Pleasant had secured enough customers to keep the equipment busy up until near snowfall.

Father and Alex were jubilant. Alex would bring the equipment to Greendale for the winter, to be parked in our stable. And Alex nearly made it. Both men had failed to take into account the high hill of white sand that at our end began at Spring Brook, within yards of Alex's house, and continued to a crest, then descending to normalcy a quarter mile beyond. The hill was a complete barrier to heavy loads that could not be carried into or out of Greendale in the winter on snow. Nowhere, short of the Sahara, could sand be found so deep, so uncontrollable, and so conducive to lusty cuss words. We had brought in heavy loads, but only in winter and on snow.

Father had a way out: Pull the machines off the road and build a shelter around them, to be proof against snow, rain and wind. Construction of the structure would be in the hands of Alex.

The harvesting equipment served with success through the first part of the following season. Then one day Father and Alex were given an offer for the machines by a farmer near Mount Pleasant. A deal was completed, and to the immense relief of the two men.

Greendale, as we found it upon moving into our home, had seemed to hold promise of a full realization of Father's dreams for a future home for his family. The land between our house and Potter Creek was under cultivation, and in the region of the creek a fair yield of barley promised well for the region. Back of our wagon shed, however, there began a rise of ground that told another story. Let a wind, even of modest proportions, come along, and an excavation to a depth of a foot and more would be left, extending to distances of fifty, even seventy-five feet. Nothing that Father could plant served to bind the soil to the earth.

The men the O'Donnell boys knew were a husky but kind-hearted lot. They occasionally worked with them, and never did they hear a man give a cuss word, although they played many a boy-like trick on them.

COURTESY OF MAITLAND C. DESORMO

Back of the barn, as far west as our back line, a half mile away, the story was little less doleful. In good time the land across the road was cleared for farming. For the first year or two, crops were fair, although here too success was achieved at the cost of excessive fertilization, but always we would be at the mercy of nature's leaching processes.

It was thus that Father's enthusiasm for Greendale as a final home for his children would be slowly a way could be found to make it blossom like the rose of ancient legend.

Chapter Twenty-two

Shivaree

SADIE'S enthusiasm for summer teaching had seemed to wane as the term progressed. A log shanty, when a torrid sun beats down on its sloped, low roof of black tarpaper, rates imperceptibly above a blast furnace. Sadie moreover must have discovered in short time that she had no prodigies among her charges. "A lot of them," I heard her tell Mother one day, "don't know B from bullfrogs."

© R.P. Nadeau

LIFE IN A
NORTH WOODS
LUMBER CAMP

Sadie thereupon began a subtle program for winter terms for the school. Her first assault on Father's ideas on the subject was to advance the argument that no boys in the district would be old enough to work in the woods for another three or four years anyhow, so why not give them enough schooling, and at times other than summer, to enable them to write their names?

Father at last succumbed to Sadie's arguments, which turned out to be the key log that loosed an entire jam of his notions on the practices of pedagogy.

Almost before we knew it, plans were under way for a term of winter schooling. Two weeks later a project was mapped out to put up a school building of hewn logs. A site was selected, at the corner where the road turned east toward the Gibbs neighborhood. Within a week the structure was being erected.

Sadie's motives could not be questioned. It had become obvious by this time that her Greendale days were near an end. Recently returning from weekends at home, she had been driven to Greendale by a young man, a tall, blond young farmer who the following Friday would be on hand to drive her home. Nobody was surprised, therefore, when one day she announced her engagement, the wedding to be held immediately after the close of the term. The announcement came at supper, and I asked if she couldn't be married here so that we could have a shivaree.

At the time I was passing through an ardent shivaree phase. Tom Bradley, Father's rollway man, in order to be all set for the ardors of the coming season in camp, had returned a few weeks before for the purpose of running up a shanty to which he could bring his bride. The announcement brought an unlooked-for result: It inspired Mother to ask why Tom couldn't have his wedding in our house.

And wedding there it was, when the shanty was finished and, with Mother's help, furnished. The young lady, Lizzie Allen, from up near Gladwin, was brought in and subjected to the expert appraisal of Mother and Sadie. After looking her over, Mother must have wondered why she had gone to so much trouble. Sadie, I think, put Lizzie in the same intellectual category with John Wilsey and me.

Father, who a year or so before had added to his many distinctions that of Justice of the Peace, was to splice the couple, and Fred and Will Jones went around the sparse community drumming up volunteers for a shivaree. Fred tried to get over to me the general idea, succeeding only in convincing me that if Jake Wilsey was coming with his circular saw, it would be for the purpose of sawing the bride and groom in two. For this I went all out.

Around eight o'clock, when supper was over and Lizzie had helped with the dishes, the knot was tied. Lizzie was dressed fit to kill in a brown gingham dress, and her hair, arranged mostly in a prodigious knot at the top of her head, had bangs that hung practically to her eyebrows. Mother, who was a great hand with geraniums and begonias, contrived a bouquet, which Lizzie, between sobs during the ceremony, kept sniffling into.

At a moment that for some reason or other seemed appropriate to Father, the bride and bridegroom arranged themselves in front of the front door, Fred and Sadie standing up with them. Facing them was Father, in all the majesty of a boiled shirt, from which, the evening being warm, he had removed the widespread ascot tie. As you followed Father, who had made this concession to the state of the weather, you couldn't decide upon which to center your attention, the Adam's apple or the gold studs that decorated the shirt bosom.

It required but a minute or two for Father to get the pair married. The ceremony was followed by an interval during which the couple were bantered by one and all, creating an atmosphere calculated to discourage any general kissing of the bride, even had anybody wanted to.

Fred, as a result of his part in the ceremonies, was in a state of complete collapse and, to get himself in shape for the doings to follow, went outdoors and stretched out on top of the woodshed, always his favorite spot for resting from the ardors of a typical Greendale day. For myself, I emerged from the scene with but one idea, which was to get hitched to Nora at the first possible moment.

At a decent hour, the happy couple left for their shanty, just across from Father's blacksmith shop, and within a half hour Jake Wilsey came out of the darkness, followed by Alex Jones, the two bearing Jake's huge circular saw mounted on a crowbar.

Will Jones turned up with a conch shell, used by his mother for notifying the family that dinner was ready and therefore, shake a leg. Two or three muzzle-loading shotguns were in the gathering, and an assortment of handbells. Fred deserved some kind of prize for thinking of the string of sleigh bells, which hung, summer and winter, on a wooden peg back of Powder Face's stall. Most doleful of all the

Work horses skidded as many as 200 logs a day. It may be readily understood, therefore, that this was not an easy day's work for man or beast.

COURTESY OF GEORGE SHAUGHNESSY

contraptions was a mouth organ, its sweet notes lost in the din led by Jake Wilsey's saw.

Soon the lamp in the happy couple's shanty was doused; a moment of utter silence followed, when suddenly Alex Jones struck a match as a signal and what Sadie next day said was bedlam suddenly had broken out. The banging of a hammer against Jake's saw, the roar of shotguns, Will's conch, Fred's sleigh bells and the laughter and yells!

> ...suddenly Alex Jones struck a match as a signal and what Sadie next day said was bedlam suddenly had broken out. The banging of a hammer against Jake's saw, the road of shotguns, Will's conch, Fred's sleigh bells and the laughter and yells!

Following the initial outburst of sound and fury, the bride and groom did not let on for a time that they were so much as aware of our proximity. In a decent time, however, a lamp went on and then, unlatching the door, the pair exhibited themselves on the little stoop and everybody came up and shook hands with, as Father put it, the happy pair, all indulging in pleasantries more or less appropriate to the occasion.

This could have been an appropriate ending to the occasion, but more was to come. Mother, who always thought of everything, and Sadie joined the group, bearing huge dripping pans of molasses and other cakes. Immediately behind them came Pat Moran with a kettle of hot coffee.

A full hour passed before the celebrants said good-bye to Tom and Lizzie, all completely tuckered out.

When Sadie left at the end of her term, the new schoolhouse was up. The men of the neighborhood, glad to help, had cut and hewn the logs, and Father had announced a raising for a day along in early October. Again all of the men of the neighborhood responded, joined by Will Conrad and Bert Gibbs and two or three others driving up from the Gibbs settlement.

Pat was up early to have the horses fed and curried, and one of the teams harnessed and ready for the big ceremonies. Father bossed the proceedings, the long sleeves of his red undershirt, projecting below the rolled-up sleeves of his flannel shirt, giving him, I thought, a commanding look as he waved his arms to indicate to the workers just where a log should go, and whether a wall was going up plumb.

The fact is that I was pretty confused by all the excitement, and when John Wilsey came up and said whatcha say we go over to the woods and get some wintergreen berries, I was all for the idea. When we returned an hour later, having gone down to the Salt for a swim and scared up a flock of partridges, the building operations had proceeded to two or three logs above the plates, each log drawn up into place by one of our teams.

Frank Bradley, acting as teamster, made a great to-do about this part of the business. When he gave the word, the horses, on the opposite side of the building from where the log was to go into place, leaned into their collars; the rope tightened ever so gradually and the log began to move up the skids, slowly, steadily, men with pike poles and peaveys holding them even, and other men making certain that the skids did not slip.

Day's end came laggardly, as signaled by Arnie blowing on our conch. By noon tomorrow, the walls would be up, and from that point on the job would be for a mason and a couple of carpenters to be brought in from the outside. These men would chink the logs and over the chinking apply plaster; joists would be sawn and put in place for floor and ceiling, and rafters for the roof. Doors and window openings would be cut, and so on until the glorious structure would be finished and ready for the opening of school.

Then one day word from Shepherd told of a shipment of freight that had arrived from Grand Rapids. Father drove out for it and when next morning the crates were unpacked in front of the schoolhouse, twelve double seats, each a cracker jack, just like they had in the city schools, were unveiled. And there were a desk for the teacher and a set of wall maps, the kind of maps you pulled down and moved up on rollers with springs, a potbelly stove and a huge bell to put up in the belfry.

The seats, when installed, were arranged six in a row on either side of the room, beginning in the back with the larger ones, and ending down front with the smallest for the likes of me. Between the two rows, well back, was placed the tall heating stove, with chrome-colored fittings. At two or three intervals was a length of wire with a turn around the pipe that would keep it from crashing down upon any kids who at the moment might be attempting to soak up wisdom from the First or Second reader.

The teacher's desk was set upon a low platform running the width of the room. In front of it was a bench upon which classes sat while going through the throes of a recitation. The only concession to memories of the former school was the woodbox, which was brought over from the shanty and put in the corner to the right of the door as one entered the building. A civic calamity was avoided when Fred prevailed upon Father to install a larger blackboard than the one in the shanty, one if possible with few knots.

The term opened late in October, and what with sitting comfortably at the shiny oak desks and staring in wonder at the maps, showing the very places that old John Bugby had us singing about, my mind was made up, as I told Edith Sweeting, our teacher, never to leave the dam place. My scholastic performance thus far must have convinced her that I had something there.

Chapter Twenty-three

Ants and Lunch Pails

FRED AND I, when school had opened in the new building, began to discuss dinner pails, Fred reminding me that we were the only kids that had never carried our dinner. While we dashed home for a meal, the other children were gathered here and there outdoors, as they ate comparing one another's pickles and cakes, and trading a slice of brown bread for a piece of berry pie.

By the time we were back at the schoolhouse, everybody would have finished his meal and be off somewhere, the girls hunting flowers and the boys down on Black Creek or the river, throwing stones at crabs and stone-rollers.

"And all we can do is wait for the bell to ring and see the kids come tearing in from the fun they've been having." Fred, I could see, was bitter about the situation.

"But we can eat with Miss Sweeting!" Some word would of course be expected of me.

© R.P. Nadeau

LIFE IN A
NORTH WOODS
LUMBER CAMP

Fred admitted that Miss Sweeting was pretty swell all right, young like Sadie but bushels prettier, the new teacher having soft, chestnut hair and blue eyes, and always laughing when away from the school. At home she played with us children, yet in school next day would stand Fred or me in the corner as soon as she would John Wilsey.

Our uneasiness was not relieved by new reports of evil doings by some of our favorite children. Millie Green mopping up the floor with True Hodgins! And Rosie Hart finding in her dinner pail upon opening it a live frog! To be told of such glamorous goings-on while we were having a quiet lunch at home was more than Fred and I could endure, and Mother did not seem surprised when one day we asked why couldn't we tote our lunch too.

Mother, it was clear, had been expecting this. "I have a better plan," she replied—"to have Pat take your lunch to you each noon. In that way you could have your things hot, and—"

"But that isn't stylish," Fred broke in, and Mother, trying to suppress her laughter, dashed from the room.

This business of taking your lunch to school had advantages that we had never dreamed of. Each pupil had a nail, driven into the wall, for holding his hat and coat, in such months as he wore them, and on it he managed to hang his dinner pail as well. You started in on your lunch at the morning recess. The early class in reading had taken a lot out of you, and your waning strength would have to be reinforced by one of the two hard-boiled eggs, and maybe a slice of bread and butter.

At noon you and Nora would sit at the end of the stoop and compare notes on the viands your respective mothers had fixed up. And maybe you traded half of your pie for a go at her cake.

In spring, at the right time, should spring ever show up, you would get Mother to put a cup in the pail, with sugar in the bottom. You started for school a half hour early and planned a descent upon a patch of wild strawberries you had stumbled into the day before.

A lunch pail filled so lavishly with sweet things as yours would have the disadvantage of being a great drawer of ants. You would mention the menace of ants to Mother, and she would take it up with the folks in Shepherd who sold pails. Relief never came from any source, a fact that

Author Tom O'Donnell, who in his early life in the 1880s, acquired considerable lumbering and river-driving understanding in Michigan's northern woods.

mattered not at all. The berries, to my taste, were just as nice when you had picked off the ants as they would have been before becoming anted.

After lunch, and before school was called for the afternoon session, you would have with the others a whirl at pom-pom-pull-away, or hide-and-seek, and maybe Miss Sweeting would let you wash the blackboard and slates. And if somebody had beaten you to that you might be permitted to pull the long bell rope that came from the belfry through an augur hole bored through the ceiling, thus bringing the rest of the kids tearing in for the afternoon exercises.

All this, what with staying nights after school, made me practically a denizen of the schoolroom. Completely overwhelmed by the glamour of the new furnishings, I determined never to leave, and Mother declared that the way I was headed I would make it. Nights after school I flatly refused to go home. I was aided in my determinations by the vigilance of Miss Sweeting, who, the first afternoon, caught me in the act of clipping True Hodgins on the ear with my ruler. For this I was penalized by being kept after school for a full half hour. What with washing the blackboard and sweeping the floor, the time passed so quickly that I asked Miss Sweeting if I might not stay on for another half hour. With a remark that the punishment was hurting her more than it did me, she said yes, but be sure to come home in time for supper.

"Fred will bring it to me, I betcha!" I declared.

Immediately I set out upon a series of investigations during which I practically wore out the wall maps, first pulling down the one dealing with North America and, after admiring ecstatically the beautiful colors, I turned to wondering where Michigan was. I finally located it in the general region of Athabasca.

Roused from my researches by a step on the porch, I looked up to see old Pat coming through the door carrying a small basket. It was my supper.

"Your ma says, says she, she will sind over fer ye a bed, says she!" said Pat.

This was more like it, and when I said yes, Pat, controlling what must have been an impulse to belt me over the head with his cane, turned and went out.

I finished the last ginger cookie as night was closing in and, no one having turned up with the bed, I concluded that Fred had started out with it but had fallen off the bridge into Black Creek. This needed looking into and I set out for the creek. Fred was not in the creek, and I determined to find him, no matter where my search might take me. I kept straight on and to my amazement I turned up at the house, where he was at the supper table asking Emory Lewis to pass the butter.

My devotion to scholarly research continued for a week, my persistence causing the family to wonder how long I could keep it up. The end came mercifully when I found the school agog one morning over a fistic battle between Joe Hart and True Hodgins on the way home from school the night before. It could not have been a battle to compare with the Sullivan-Kilrain bout, since Joe could only display a scratch along the left side of his face and a touch of sulk in his manner. It was a battle, however, and that settled it for me. That afternoon I joined the after-school procession homeward.

Fred, apparently feeling that the occasion called for another battle, went into a huddle with Will Jones when we were just nicely getting under way. Presently Fred declared, in a voice everybody could hear, that Tom could too lick the socks offen John Wilsey. Will said he betcha John could lick the socks offen Tom, if he had any on.

John and I bridled at the challenges built up for us and went to work. We glared at each other, we shot dares and double dares each other's way, and we taunted and vaunted. By this time we had got around to clenching our fists; cautiously, each with popping eyes glued on the other, we inched towards each other until, finally convinced that there was no way out of it, we let go with everything we had, such as it was.

Before long we were each having the other in the dirt, first one and then the other on top, snarling anathemas, each spitting in the other's face, throwing punches with the utmost abandon and wondering if it wasn't near suppertime. There would come a time of complete exhaustion and we got off the ground, found our dinner pails and proceeded on our way. The battle of course would be resumed the next evening.

Never did Fred and I leave the group to turn in at our house. Always we went as far at least as Potter Creek. The things most needing our attentions, indeed, lay at the creek. A period had to be devoted to jumping off the bridge onto the soft, damp sand below, in a contest to see which kid could, with a running jump, catapult himself off the bridge in a wide, sweeping arc and land farthest from the bridge. And on days when it rained, a dam had to be built in the ditch that ran alongside the road and sent its water cascading down the bank to the creek below.

The trick was for each boy, when a sizable head of water had accumulated behind the dam, to drop in a stick, preferably a piece of dry pine, then tear out the dam and see whose ship survived the mad, plunging flood and would be the first to reach the creek.

Besides these excitements, there were always fish darting about in the creeks, fairly asking for a rock-throwing contest, or else standing by for the daily emptying of crumbs from dinner pails.

> ...running tight as ever we could we would peel off our clothes as we ran in order that, arriving at the swimming hole, and still on the run, we could drop our clothes in a heap, take the final long step and plunge into the depths below.

In most of these activities, except the punching of noses, the girls took part along with the boys. Come spring, with warmer water in the streams, on the other hand, a new routine was added from which the ladies were barred—a run for the swimming hole, which was reached by leaving the highway a dozen rods beyond the Potter Creek bridge and tearing lickety-split to our swimming hole, a good twenty rods from the road. The Salt had made two or three sharp turns, and in this last one it went all out. The turn here was so sharp that a fairly long, deep hole had been worn out and to get into it you made a long, horizontal dive from the bank, or slid, sitting up, down the five or six feet of clay. The long dive obviously was the means preferred by all of the adherents of Salt River swimming.

From the time we left the female members of the going-home group of children it was ritual to say, "Betch I'll be the first one in!" To achieve that distinction, running tight as ever we could we would peel off our clothes as we ran in order that, arriving at the swimming hole, and still on the run, we could drop our clothes in a heap, take the final long step and plunge into the depths below.

There we would paddle around, swim a few strokes now and then, until at the top of our voices we would yell, "See me dive with my eyes open!" only to see a monstrous crawfish coming at us. Soon we would be splashing water on the sloping blue-clay bank, making it so slippery that, sitting bolt upright, we could slide down and go kersplash in the water. Scarcely waiting to catch a fresh breath we would go back, rubbing places that smarted on nether areas and extracting abrasive pebbles that somehow had become imbedded in the clay.

When these and other routines had been repeated, time and again, Fred would say it was about suppertime, kid, what say we hurry home. When finally we had dressed and were turning back into the road I could hardly wait until I went to school next morning so that we could go swimming at night. I was now as determined never to hang around the school a minute after closing time as previously I had been never to leave the dam place.

Chapter Twenty-four

Camp 19

THE PREVIOUS December our blacksmith had made for me and to my size a glamorous peavey, which awaited me Christmas morning beneath a glittering tree. The gift was accepted as a sign that, in Santa's mind at least, I was growing up. It was essentially a river driver's implement, and I would keep it in mothballs until high water brought the spring drive.

© R.P. Nadeau

LIFE IN A
NORTH WOODS
LUMBER CAMP

Time passed so fast in Greendale, with so many things always to be done, that the break-up was upon us suddenly and the peavey fairly calling upon me for action. Action, however, would have to wait until the high water had given way to a lower stage within the banks of the river.

Fred already was a competent rider of logs, which meant among other things that he could ride out a burling log with the best of them, providing the size of the log had some relation to his weight. I would never be in Fred's class, but with one of Bob Williams's peavies, I had an ambition someday to take part in one of Father's drives.

So it was that when water was back within the banks of the Salt, I found a stranded log that called to me to get it on its way to Saginaw. It was a simple job to cant and roll the log into a backwash of the stream, hop aboard, push myself into the current and so be launched upon a dream career.

Holding my peavey horizontally in front of me, heels in and toes out, I gripped the log firmly with my feet. In a brave attempt at an easy stance, all according to standard procedure, I broke into a lumberwoods chanty that for some reason was approved singing for men on the drive:

> *I saw a ship go 'round the bend,*
> *Good-by, my lover, good-by,*
> *It was loaded down with Midland men,*
> *Good-by, my lover, good-by.*
> *By-o, by baby...*

The "Midland" had loyal reference to our county. The third line was varied to the extent that the song was used in just about any place and situation. In the second Cleveland campaign, it was put to wide use in our region to the extent that we heard variously of Cleveland men and Harrison men who loaded down the ship, with little concern for party affiliations. With appropriate changes the song was popular among railway men, both of the Flint & Pere Marquette and the Toledo & Ann Arbor lines.

My own craft came suddenly to a bend, where the current turned so sharply as to surprise my log and set it burling. The situation sent me into a cold sweat, as the saying was, when it suddenly came to me that I had no calks in my boots—for that matter I did not have on adequate river footwear.

No real driver would ever venture upon a log without his calked boots, and a profound impression of this fact, more probably than fear, added to my confusion. I was going to ride it out, however, and I tried to out-spin the log and wear it down. Its momentum only increased, and up to the point where my feet could go no faster. Suddenly I was overboard and in the drink (what riverman would ever think of using the word "river"?) dog-fashioning it for shore. Mercifully, the water was not deep.

I was retrieved by "Jew's-Harp" Wilson and later the peavey was recovered by Fred.

Out of the spirit that led us to prefer homemade toys must have grown the instinct that turned us to games of our own contriving, a top-flight example of which was "Camp 19." The numeral 19 must have been drawn out of a hat—at least I never heard any meaning that would explain the number. Fred, our imaginative leader, would of course have selected it.

Camps, more often than not, were known by the names of their owners. Ours was "O'Donnell's Camp," and a few miles away was a "Higgins' Camp," and still nearer was the site of what had been "Gordon's Camp," owned by William D. Gordon, Midland attorney, who years later represented the District in Congress.

There were also camps designated by numbers, and somehow "14" or "17" stirred our imaginations as a mere name could never do. Most of the cases of violence in camps that we boys heard of seemed to occur in places bearing mysterious numerals. Obviously, so prosaic a designation as a mere name would never do for our camp, and number it was—number 19. By the time we got this detail settled, snow had come, and immediately we embarked upon the great adventure.

Black Creek was settled as the center of our operations. The Black, as Greendale wisecracking kids had it, could be negotiated in two jumps. It rose somewhere to the northwest in Isabella County, and by the time it reached our home it had attained a width of but five or six feet in its broader spots. It was an exceedingly winding stream, combinations of two and three ox-bow turns across the width of its valley being common, and straight-aways of 30 feet unknown.

On one of its sudden turns, where the bank dropped two full feet into the creek, we established our rolling bank. This would receive our logs as they were cut by the crew and drawn in from the scene of cutting operations.

A rollway, presenting tier after tier of logs, dozens of them, each piled high with row upon row of logs, was always a sight to stir the heart. We were resolved, even if we did not debate the subject, that Camp 19 would present a rollway that would live up to the finest of lumbering traditions.

Back a quarter of a mile from the creek the heavy timber gave way to a small opening where younger growths of pine and hemlock grew in profusion. There would be the scene of our sawing operations. To reach it we built a logging road, achieved by much whacking away of underbrush and the grubbing down of high spots of ground into the low spots.

All the boys in the neighborhood had been assigned (by Fred, who of course was the foreman of "19") their parts in the enterprise. Bud and True Hodgins were naturals for service as the team of lusty sorrels. Fred was the teamster, and right merrily did he carry on, calling out his gees and haws to the cracking of a blacksnake whip, which he had appropriated from Father's supply of persuaders.

John Wilsey was put at one end of our crosscut saw, and Joe Hart at the other. This arrangement John accepted with becoming grace. Nobody

As far as the eye could see, the river was dotted with the smooth-moving logs—until a jam formed. Then the lumber stopped its downriver journey. The logs piled up, one atop the other, stacking in hodge-podge fashion like gigantic jackstraws. Then it was up to the drivers, those skilled, nimble-footed woodsmen, to disentangle the pile that towered 30 or 40 feet above the surface of the water.

COURTESY OF PAT PAYNE

seemed to know much about the Harts and what compulsions had brought them into the region. Joe was a good-natured, lumbering kid of around ten years, but his personality was pretty much lost in the attention attracted by his sister Rosie, older by two years than Joe. Rosie, fair of face and fairly fair of form, demanded immediate and boisterous attention by an eye that wheeled about in a wide orbit of its own.

Camp 19 had its notcher, too, a job that fell to Will Jones. Will's capacities fitted him for a place less lowly, though looking back upon our fun I can see that Fred's confidence in Will's resourcefulness was nothing if not inspired. In his hands, the job of notcher attained a state little short of sublimity. He saw to it that trees fell in places requiring complete ambidexterity of the sawyers, and in addition the utmost in agility. John Wilsey came in one night insisting that to saw one log he and True Hodgins were obliged to stand on their heads.

For rosser I was selected, out of consideration, I surmise, for my tender age. My only qualification was a boundless enthusiasm for my work, in the performance of which I set an all-time high, since I refused to leave a log until it was entirely denuded of its bark. My tenure in that particular job was not of long duration. Fred, his aesthetic sense outraged, declared that bare logs did not look too good. I suspect the real reason was that it was difficult to keep his place on top of a load of slippery, barkless logs when riding over the uncertain road to the rollway.

> Our "camp" and the hours of fun that grew out of it were not conducive to instilling in the monds of the young lumbermen a high devotion to the principles of conservation, for in the interest of fun we did away with a lot of potential forest.

A job that Fred had not filled was that of swamper, and the swamper's horses, all to be performed by one person. This fell to Allie Farr. Allie accepted the post with a good deal of alacrity, but his ardor cooled when he found that he had to help out in rossing at such times as shaking ague had me flat on my back.

It is pleasant to report that Allie rose to the occasion, displaying a positive genius in keeping his various functions apart. Driving himself up to a log, skittish and leaping frantically at the slightest noise, he somehow contrived to hold himself in check long enough to tie a rope around an end of a log for snaking to the skidway, for we had no dray. Adjusting the other end of the rope about his shoulders, he would lean into an imaginary collar, champ at an imaginary bit and shout to himself, "Geddap, Prince! Geddap, Fan!"

A minute of terrific struggle would follow, but suddenly the two-foot loglet, all of four or five inches thick, would begin to move, ever so little at first, but at last actually on its way to the skidway. Arrived there, Allie would draw up at the lower end of the skidway, unhitch the rope and, detaching himself masterfully from his dual role of team and driver, roll the log to the elevated front end of the skidway, ready to be loaded on the sleigh on one of Fred's early trips.

Our "camp" and the hours of fun that grew out of it were not conducive to instilling in the minds of the young lumbermen a high devotion to the principles of conservation, for in the interest of fun we did away with a lot of potential forest.

Chapter Twenty-five

Timber

© R.P. Nadeau

LIFE IN A
NORTH WOODS
LUMBER CAMP

CAMP 19 got off to a flying start, thanks especially to its sawyers, who applied themselves to their task with an enthusiasm that threatened to annihilate Greendale's entire sapling population. The notcher, who tried desperately to get the trees ready for the sawyers, dug in and swung his ax with might and main, but always the sawyers stood behind him telling him to get a hump on. The poor rosser, who then had to get each log ready for snaking to the skidway, was doing his frantic best to keep ahead of the sawyers.

All in all, the camp threatened to break all production records in Michigan's biggest industry. Fortunately, the fury of the attack was quickly spent. The schedule of Camp 19 provided that our operations should be carried out only on Saturdays and evenings after school. Since our first feverish burst of activity took place on a Saturday, Fred, who in addition to being teamster was also foreman of the outfit, would have time to think up some way of allaying the energy of John Wilsey and Joe Hart.

Nature fortunately stepped in. John came down with mumps and Joe turned up at school on Monday with something that he diagnosed as charley horse.

Here was a clear break for the rest of us. We pitched in and, by diligent application every night after school, nightfall the following Saturday saw the last of the vast accumulation of logs unloaded from the sleigh at the rollway on Black Creek.

By this time Fred had begun to worry about banking space at the rollway. Already the banking ground, as the result of Bunyanesque energies, was more than half-filled. Thereafter, until the mumps subsided at John's house, we busied ourselves in building a second banking ground at the next bend in the creek, a few yards further down. This meant a corresponding extension of the road, occasioning a noisy whacking away at brush and filling in low spots and grading down high ones with pickaxes and shovels that we had appropriated from Father's equipment.

At this point it suddenly dawned on Fred that Camp 19 had no marking iron. Unless our logs were properly marked, what was to keep some other lumberman from branding our logs with his iron and selling them along with his own? True asked what other lumberman, and Fred answered him with a look that froze him in his tracks.

The entire gang, acting as a committee of the whole, waited upon our blacksmith and explained the situation. Solemnly the smith said that he saw our point, thought our stand very well taken indeed, and what would be our mark? Father's mark was 4-bar-D and Fred, after going into a huddle with the rest of the crew, asked how about D-bar 4?

This was a perfectly wonderful idea, according to the blacksmith. And when could he have it finished and ready for delivery? Would six o'clock be in time? It would, but it wasn't. Half the crew played hooky that afternoon and converged on the blacksmith shop, where we displayed new and fantastic ways of being constantly underfoot, directing the blacksmith's endeavors. It was noon of the next day that the entire gang dashed to the shop when school was out. The beautiful instrument was placed in Fred's hands, and that evening was put to lusty use.

In this department, our technique was far from orthodox. At Father's rollways you went up to a log and just whammed away. We had a problem all our own, as Fred explained. Wham away at the end of one of our little logs, and it would go sailing into the middle of next week. Will Jones said why not stand on the log and then wham away—in regular camps the man with the marker always stood on a log when he whammed. Will's logic was beyond reproach, and a compromise was reached by having Bud Hodgins stand on the log and Fred do the whamming.

Will picked up the first log and laid it where Fred would have a clear field, unhampered by bushes, for his swing. Bud at last got himself balanced on the log, swaying this way and that, since the log had a tendency to burl even on dry land. Suddenly, when all was still, Fred let go with the iron. The log, however, shot out from under Bud, who was whammed into the middle of the creek. Wet and shivery, Bud was retrieved from the icy drink, as mad, he always said afterward, as a hornet.

The truth is that Bud was madder than that even. In his eye was the look of mayhem, and his eye fell on me as a likely victim. Without a word of explanation or by your leave, he whammed away with a blow that landed in an eye. The battle that followed was as indecisive and as painless as were all of our struggles, and when order restored itself our marking problem was easily solved by standing a log on one end on the ground, Will Jones holding it and Fred whamming away. Shades of Paul Bunyan!

This and the episode that followed should be cited by lecturers on management as a classic example of careful and complete planning. The logs, all properly D-bar-4'd, were barely back in pretty tiers on the rollway when Allie Farr observed with consummate casualness:

"Gosh all fishhooks, Fred, when're we goin' to scale them there logs?"

Here was something else that had been left out of our plans. Fred, fortunately, was equal to the occasion and said we would do it right away. Already it was Saturday noon, but next week would not be soon enough. Reminding the crew that "Now!" was our motto, a bit of news to us all,

Fred dashed to the house and returned with a partially-filled memorandum book that Father had discarded, the remains of an ancient pencil, and a broken-down log rule.

Logs were moved on sleighs from the woods to the mills or to streams where they could be floated to the mills.

In the meantime, the rest of us were retrieving the logs from the creek and stacking them like cordwood on the bank. This made us wet and cold all over again. The only complaint heard, however, was when Will Jones said that gosh, if we kept on handling them logs much more we'd havum worn clean out.

The broken-down log rule had, of course, no provision for two-foot logs like ours, a fact that had no meaning for Greendale's greatest improviser. Applying the ruler across the end of a log, and putting his finger on it at the point of the rim, he would hold the ruler close to his eyes and after a minute's deliberation call out, "Fourteen!" a major exaggeration if ever there had been one in Greendale.

True Hodgins, book in hand, and serving as the scaler's helper, jotted something down in the book—something that no one ever cared to consult.

At long last, the rollway was back in place and I was streaking for home, by now a wet and shivering mass. Fred saw me.

"Hey, you with the yeller mackinaw, where you goin'?"

"Home! I'm all tuckered out!" I replied.

"What's the pucker? Come back here and help carry the tools!" he called.

I came back, thoroughly cowed, shouldered a pike pole, the only object that wasn't already on somebody's shoulder, and fell in at the end of the line. This spot put me in a position of imminent danger to all in front. Luckily the only casualty was Will Jones, just in front of me. As I swayed in an effort to climb over a log Will caught the pike end of the pole in the region of the left ear, he with emotion suggesting that I carry that dam pole the other end to. In the process of making the shift suggested by Will, I clipped him one in the region of the other ear, reducing him, for the first time in his life without doubt, to complete silence.

Rosie! That gave me an idea. He had been wrestling with the problem of finding a scaler, since our supply of boys wouldn't stretch that far. Why not give Rosie the scaler job?

Fred and I, bushed by the exertions of the day, fell asleep at the supper table, I just after my plate of pork and beans and Fred, foreman of the outfit and therefore made of sterner stuff, at the end of his dried-apple pie.

Next morning Fred was explaining to Father the problems that brought concern to a foreman of a camp like "19."

"And then John Wilsey gets the mumps and Dan's wing goes back on him, and not a stick of timber cut since—"

I caught a wink that Father passed to Mother.

"I can tell you how to catch up on your sawing, Fred. Next spring when the creek breaks up, you drive your logs down as far as the bridge and run them into a boom there and I will buy them from you. I will pay you ten dollars for every thousand feet, and you and your crew divide the money between you."

Fred, I could see, was tempted by the offer—it would give him some extra Fourth of July money. Then his thoughts turned sadly to John and Dan and what they would do in production with so great an incentive before them. Finally, with a knowing look toward me, he said no, he'd be gosh darned if he would; he'd marry Rosie Hart first.

Rosie! That gave me an idea. He had been wrestling with the problem of finding a scaler, since our supply of boys wouldn't stretch that far. Why not give Rosie the scaler job?

This was inspiration at its best. Fred admitted it in so many words, and next morning he made the appointment. Rosie was probably the only lady surveyor in the history of the industry. Her calculations were often astonishing, as when she measured one log at 37,000 feet and had to ask Fred how to write it out.

There were times when our enthusiasms waned, but our chief managed to keep the operation going until the spring break-up. Altogether we had eleven rollways filled with our logs. To find so many proper sites, we were obliged to go upstream, and then cross the creek and use likely spots on the other side.

At long last came the break-up. Spring was in the air and a growing lassitude in our attack on our lumbering operation. Before we could end our season's efforts, however, we must have a drive.

A drive presented problems. Every hand would want to take part, but half of them would be in the way. Father, all sympathy when Fred explained the situation, suggested taking half of the boys for getting the drive down to the butternut tree and the others the rest of the way to the Salt. This was inspiration at its best, I let Father know.

Two days later the ice had gone out of the creek, and after school we got the drive started. A man had to be good to be a driver on the Black, I told myself. You couldn't ride logs the size of ours. And anyhow, you didn't have calks in whatever boots you were wearing, which among the boys was mostly felts and rubbers or, instead of the felts, you wore socks that came to just below the knees—which in deep snow were tied above the knees. The rubbers were "gunboats," as Mother called all heavy footwear; they had thick soles and fastened over the instep with a clasp or a buckle.

There was nothing, of course, to prevent imagining we were riding downstream on top of an unruly log, peavey in hand, burling it like old hickory until we wore it down and had it eating out of our hand.

Driving problems were many and serious, but Fred, in talking to his men, told the whole story in a few words.

> *"Your job, fellers, is to keep the logs out there in the middle
> of the drink and keepum moving. If you stop fer just a minute,
> they'll jam up on you quicker'n wildcats."*

Camp 19 came out pretty well. Most of our logs reached the Salt. Along Black Creek, however, many of our logs were left high and dry, and for years on our visits to the scene, we were coming across them, half sunken in mire in the lower places, and in others all but hidden from sight in the silt. In the bottom of the creek were dead-heads that, for one reason or another, had lacked the buoyancy to keep them afloat. Such as these of our logs were things of joy and beauty to the horned dace that darted in and out among them.

Chapter Twenty-six

Three Little Indians

NO TEACHER could ever consider the months spent in our school a total loss. She might have hours when she was homesick for her folks and friends back in Detroit or Bay City, and when she would be disturbed by seeing so many lumberjacks at so close a range and so much of the time. She might, had she been familiar with a suitable phrase, have put her charges down as a bunch of jerks. One point, however, she would have to concede: She was never bored by them.

Certainly no group of children ever displayed a spirit of more utter detachment from the whole business of learning things than did the dozen and a half of us. We were sharp enough to get by, and that was all that could be said for us. Lessons were learned with one eye on the assignment and the other on fun, mostly outside the schoolroom and not during school hours.

Fred's contributions to our fun usually took highly ingenious forms, and he was never more original than when, one noon hour, he climbed, unseen, to the roof of a lean-to

© R.P. Nadeau

LIFE IN A NORTH WOODS LUMBER CAMP

woodshed at the rear of the schoolhouse. Here he removed a board from the gable, and, a mouth organ in his pocket, crawled into the space between roof and ceiling. Only Fred, on so hot and sultry a day, would have ventured into the torrid, sweltering chamber.

In spite of the heat, Fred waited patiently, and without a sound, until an hour and more had passed. Suddenly, into the schoolroom, utterly silent, there came a low, sweet note that in imagination sounded like the notes of a hunter's horn coming to us, faint and enchanting, from a long, long way off. This was fancy at its best, since I had never heard a hunter's horn.

Suddenly the call changed to a lower and even sweeter note in the same chord. Then silence. The geography class, reciting at the time, stopped dead in its tracks, every ear in the room drinking in the lovely strains and wondering where the stuff was coming from. I whispered to John Wilsey that it was not the Day of Judgment because if it was the angel Gabriel by that time would be standing in the doorway.

At last the room was able to return to a state near normal. John was telling Miss Hickling that Chicago was situated on the Missouri River, when without warning the sweet strains came again. And again every ear was tilted to catch the full effects of the simple chord. And again, after a few minutes had passed, the school droned on in its accustomed manner.

Again and again at intervals the musical interlude was repeated until recess. At this point Fred, done to a turn by the heat, slipped out of his oven and into the brush behind the building in a wide detour, entering the schoolroom at the bell with an air of the most utter detachment. Teacher, if she suspected the truth, kept the fact to herself, and it was days before Fred let me and Will Jones in on the secret.

Except for minor forms of mischief, and particularly the wintergreen berry routines, the school was strangely well behaved. In all the years that I attended, there were no cases of flogging, unless we except perhaps the time when Nellie Gibbs set about punishing Will for putting a field mouse in her lunch pail. Fred (as a matter of course it would be Fred) was sent to cut a gad. In a swale a short distance from the school he found a lithe, straight willow that would have delighted the heart of a Hoosier schoolmaster. Fred in a number of places ringed the willow around with his knife, and so carefully that his handicraft did not show. Nellie called Will before her desk and struck in the direction of his waist only to have the stick snap into a half-dozen pieces. Fred's punishment was dismissal for the rest of the afternoon, a penalty that grieved the rest of us as much as it delighted him.

My own notable contribution to the school's lighter moments was the two little Indians. Seriously, even solemnly, the idea was conceived, and to the end on my part was carried through in much the same spirit. There were times when my little friends threatened to disrupt the entire school and give us the afternoon off.

During the winter a family of honest-to-gosh Chippewas had come in, on the river bottoms of the Salt, not far from our rollway, setting up a shelter with some of the architectural qualities of a teepee and others of a flabby canvas wall tent. Into its making had gone parts of several dated tents and patches. Skins and blankets laid on the ground served as floor and rugs, and pieces of carpeting for bed and bedding. From a fire in the middle of the room, smoke escaped through an opening in the peak. The family consisted of Papa and Mama Chippewa and Jim and Joe, two lads of near my own age.

The family's purpose for coming was to weave baskets. The river flats were covered with a rich growth of elm and basswood, and from the bark of these trees they were accumulating a kind of fortune in baskets that one day they would take to the down-river towns for selling to an unrationed public.

Father and Fred had established friendly relations with the family and never made a social call without handing over a token of their good will in the form of a slab of bacon, a loaf of Arnie's best bread, or whatever might be in the house at the time.

For myself, I remained guarded. Keep in mind it was the late 1880s. My knowledge of native people was limited to tales of the U.S. Cavalry fighting bloody battles with "the savages," and I saw no reason to doubt that our new neighbors fell into the same category, just waiting for a

chance to do us in with the tomahawks they undoubtedly kept sharp and at the ready.

The time had come, however, when curiosity could no longer hold out, and one day for the first time I entered an Indian home. I walked behind

If a buddy or friend needed a helping hand, 'jacks were always ready to help even though it may have meant contributing their last dime.

COURTESY OF *THE INDEPENDENCE*

Father, most of the time far back, constantly looking behind me to see that I was not being stalked and scanning the trees right and left to make sure that no painted warrior was lurking behind them.

Our host, if not given to prolonged talk, was friendliness itself, as was the attitude of the other members of his family. Father had told me that John, head of the family, had no other name so far as he knew, news that disappointed me, because I had supposed that all Indians were named like Sitting Bull. John talked mostly in indistinct grunts and Mary, the spouse, said nothing at all as she went ahead and plaited the thin strips of bark and listened to Father, who was an out-and-out conversationalist.

The two boys and I were soon approaching a basis, tentatively, of friendship, and when I asked them if they went to school they asked what that was. They seemed so delighted at my description of ours that I wondered if maybe I myself had not failed in appreciation of its true worth.

I asked if they would like to go to school with me some day. They said yes, but they would have to ask their father. This they did in a long session in Chippewa, and John's reply was an enthusiastic "Ugh," which apparently meant that first they would have to fix it up with my old man. The business was duly fixed up with Father, and so it was that next morning I went to school with two young Indians in tow. I properly showed off by putting on an air of extreme importance and an attitude of profound chumminess with them, aware that the other children were shaking in their boots, at any moment expecting a tomahawk to go sailing through the room and land in the bright line of Miss Hickling's hair-part.

Miss Hickling, who seemed only mildly startled, let us sit three in a seat and immediately the two young Chippewas were engrossed in my geography, particularly interested in the pictures of igloos and Northern Lights. They weren't going to let me out of their sight, however, and insisted on going with me to the recitation bench; Miss Hickling smiled and asked them questions about what the Chippewa word for "dog" was, a topic that alone occupied the rest of the recitation period, delighting the rest of the class beyond words.

The visit was so successful that Miss Hickling asked the boys to come regularly, and when I promised to teach them the ABC's in hours after school their delight was unfeigned.

Never before, probably, had the alphabet been presented with so much enthusiasm and with so little light. For a spell my newfound friends ate with me nightly, and after supper we wrestled with everything from A for apples to Z for zebras, their chubby hands drawing out the capital letters with tiresome deliberation but with little black eyes sparkling as a "G," finally finished at the cost of infinite pains, was held up by one for the other to see. They entered into the spirit of the school and took part in all of the games, becoming particularly adept at sheep-pen-down, since they could easily outrun any other boy in their class.

The importance that came to me as the sponsor of two little Chippewa friends was short-lived. Signs of spring were in the air, telling John that it was time to take to the trail. One morning Father and I went down to their camp and, after mutual declarations of affection and fidelity, the four Chippewas were off, John and Mary hauling sleds loaded with camp paraphernalia and baskets, and my two little friends with so many baskets attached to them that I expected any minute to see them take off into the stratosphere.

Chapter Twenty-seven

The Piece Across the Road

© R.P. Nadeau

LIFE IN A
NORTH WOODS
LUMBER CAMP

THE TIMBER across the road, between the house and the Salt, occupied roughly a square tract of land, bounded on two sides by the road and the river, and on the north and south sides by Black and Potter Creeks. Mother was obliged to prod Father into lumbering it, longing for a wider horizon to the east. Father made no serious objections to her wishes since the land ultimately would be cleared in any case and put into crops.

Fred and I resented the intrusion of civilization chiefly because our favorite trails would be destroyed. A path, or trail (the words were in most respects synonymous in Greendale) might be a tortuous affair, but that would be, in our practice, because Fred and my short legs would find it a simpler matter to go around a blown-down tree than to climb over it.

Two or three trails led from the house to the Salt, and one, made by Fred and me, to Potter Creek. In our first cut through the woods, headed for the creek, we had come to a swale that at the time, in spring, was covered, to the depth of several inches, with water. To get across dry-shod required a good deal of hopping from hummock to hummock. This was such good fun that thereafter, in even the driest of weather, we crossed through the low ground, although adding eight or ten rods to our distance. Beyond the swale were great trees blown down, and each we negotiated by means of a wide-circling route that soon had become part of our trail.

In such ways was a new path born, a crooked, twisting route that practically doubled for us the distance to Potter Creek at the old ford but that was something peculiarly and delightfully our own.

For Fred and me, the clearing and plowing of this piece of land was wanton destruction. Whenever in after years we visited the scene, we would spend an hour or two attempting to identify just where our trail left the highway, where it entered and left the low ground, and where it went wide around the beech tree, because we had not liked the sound of a swarm of bees crawling around on a nest hanging from a limb.

Our discovery of bees was put to early and appropriate use when, during a noon-hour, an assortment of Doubting Thomases were on their way to Potter Creek to see for themselves the lamprey eels which Fred and I always talked about when gloating was of little use in our heated discussions. Passing a tree humming with bees, we stopped and soon were standing about discussing bees in general, and with such long sticks as we could find were trying to reach the apparent location of the honey. The bees, resenting the intrusion, began flying wildly about. One, suddenly eyeing Joe Bronk, nicked the lad on a cheek. Nora Jones started to flee what promised to become a general onslaught, but was closed in upon by two of the miscreants. Other children of sterner stuff than Nora stood their ground, but one by one were knocked off until all but one of the eight intruders had been clipped—one of the Avery girls. Each of the victims, crying in pain, was dismissed for the afternoon, and a grand discovery had been made by Fred and me.

Next day during the noon hour Fred and I headed a group that included the entire student body for a look at the eels. As we approached the bee tree, Fred prevailed upon the entire group again to pause for a brush-up on bee habits. In his most eloquent manner he paused under the bee tree and began to touch eloquently upon the delight of slices of bread and butter spread thick with wild honey. Suddenly a pair of the miscreants, coming in from nowhere, clipped both of the Parsons girls, and another nipped Will Jones. The battle was on, not ending until the last child, May Wilsey, cried out from a clip above an eye.

This time, when one by one we reached the schoolhouse, crying in our pain, we were all sent home for the afternoon, and trips to see the lamprey eels had become standard student practice, until the day when Father brought in a crew to clear the area for the plow. Trees were downed and sawn into logs and the logs hauled off to the Wilsey mill; small brush was cleared away and gathered in piles for burning, these followed as the operation continued by stumps that were blasted out when they resisted the efforts of shovel and spade.

The stumps were, of course, a special problem. A hemlock stump was simple enough: Just dig a hole around and under a root, run through a chain and say "Geddap" to old Mag and Brownie and it would be out, just like that.

Pine stumps were something else, and mostly Father left them in the ground and plowed around them. Inasmuch as their roots ran about in every direction, it was difficult for the man who handled the plow, the plow-point forever catching on a root and bringing the team up with a start.

Then came an afternoon when all of these piles of debris were fired. Fred and I had a field day. The school term had ended and we could give the operations our undivided attention, assisted after a time by Will Jones and John Wilsey. Mostly John and I devoted the time to seeing who could get closest to a fire and stay longest. This meant that shortly our faces were burned to a deep red, and forced a dash down to the swimming hole, this procedure repeated until dusk inspired the musical frogs to their best efforts, efforts that had the effect of unnerving us.

The night hours of the holocaust were more glorious, if it were possible,

than the hours of daylight. The fire crackled louder at night, and try as you might you couldn't see how far up in the trees the red fire didn't go. We were in a constant dither, what with this and that, and I would not have been astonished had the angel Gabriel suddenly appeared and blown his trumpet in our ears.

Except for an acre set aside for potatoes, the new field was given over to corn. Always the first crop on newly cleared ground was supposed to be corn. Next year it would be oats: It should have been wheat, but our sandy soil was too light for wheat, according to Father, who knew about such things. After oats it would be either clover or a mixture of clover and timothy.

Fred and I were put in charge of potatoes. They could have been worked with a horse and cultivator, for we had a new cultivator and a plethora of idle horses. Fred, however, became suddenly hoe conscious and insisted that waiting upon potatoes should be in the hand of experts. Father suggested that Fred do the bugging, the truth being, Fred pointed out, that I had a way with potato bugs and that with me taking over the bugging, he could devote his entire time to hoeing.

> Running across the road he came back with a liberal sprinkling of the insects jabbed into the butter of the sandwich. Placing the other slice over it, he consumed what history, if it ever delves into the subject, must record as the first and probably only potato-bug sandwich ever eaten by man.

This suggestion of Fred's was news to me, and I could scarcely wait until the pretty pests appeared. Every morning when the potatoes had started to come up I was across the road before breakfast to see if bugs were among them. It so happened that year that when they did arrive, it was with banners. Pat Moran, with pail and the stub of a broom, sprinkled Paris Green over the plants, but the bugs only doted on what should have been their nemesis. From morning until night, I was up and among them, with a tomato can and a paddle, the bugs only browsing in greater numbers and in untold capacity for potato plants garnished with Paris Green.

I was in the midst of all this when relief came: my regular visitation of shaking ague. Old Pat took over the job of encouraging potato bugs. John

Wilsey, who had never believed in so much as the existence of the disease, came in to see me in the grip of the ague, and by good chance at a time when I was putting on one of my more brilliant exhibitions. He looked on in silence at my performance. When the attack was over and the bed had ceased rattling, he said, "Gee but that was fun. Do it again, Tom!"

John intimated to Mother that a "piece" would not be amiss, and when she brought a sandwich there followed shortly one of the most spectacular and useless feats of all gastronomic time. John was asking what started the ague anyhow and I told him potato bugs. Just one of my casual observations.

"Aw," he said, "I et some once and they didn't make me shake none!"

I objected that eating them was different from knocking them into tomato cans and anyways, I bet he couldn't do it again.

He would show me. Running across the road he came back with a liberal sprinkling of the insects jabbed into the butter of the sandwich. Placing the other slice over it, he consumed what history, if it ever delves into the subject, must record as the first and probably only potato-bug sandwich ever eaten by man. Mother, when I told her of the feat, was horrified, gave John a glass of water, and told him to run home and quickly. Next morning he was back, looking exceedingly fit, a condition that commended the diet to me.

Autumn came, and for the benefit of history it may be recorded that the corn and potatoes had done themselves proud. The potatoes were put by, part in the cellar but most of them in pits.

While all of this was going on, Father had neighbors in to help cut the corn and a couple of weeks later to husk it. Father during the summer had built a granary near the tool shop, thus fitting it in with the general scheme of the quadrangle. Bins built into it received the grain soon after the husking.

Our herd of cows was never a large one. At no time did we have more than eight cows, but since most of our butter was brought from Midland, wooden pails filled with it, the cows yielded enough milk to answer the needs of growing children and cooking, with sufficient left over for a lift to our butter supply.

The chief difficulty in the arrangement lay in the fact that the supply of milk was heaviest in summer, a time when the population of our camps was barely existent. The surplus, however, was a boon to Arnie's pride, who claimed that back on the farm she was the most expert hand in the neighborhood in salting down, a statement that always brought a smile into Mother's eyes. All I remember is that she used up for butter storage all of the wooden pails brought, filled with butter, from Midland.

It should be recorded that not a little milk went into the making of Dutch cheese, which Mother always declared was just dandy for growing children. Be that as it may, we never tired of the dish, revealing a taste on our part that would have inspired Professor Metchnikoff to the greatest heights of eloquence in his praise of lactic acid products.

What with building the new granary, getting the corn and cornstalks in, and making sure the cows were not neglected, the barnyard that summer was a busy place. There was the care of the horses, too, though this activity had gone on in all previous summers. Horses and their care received more of Fred's and my thoughts during the months in which the lumberjacks were absent. One of the jobs which thrilled us was the riding of them, three times a day, to Potter Creek for watering. For this we had worked out a technique that embraced mounting the horses in their stalls.

Dropping the halter from Bay Prince, for example, we lay stretched along his back, arms draped around his neck. A signal for him to dash out of his stall, and he scooted under the low door, with so little clearance that one of Greendale's great mysteries was how we escaped having our heads bashed in. Then came the dash to the creek and the return run, the horses slowing down inches short of the doorjamb and sliding inside.

All this gave us five trips each watering time, or fifteen for the day— thirty escapes by a squeak of having a head bashed in.

Hay, even after we began to grow things, had to be bought and brought in for the horses. We hadn't far to go for it—five and six miles would take us into a rich farming region out beyond Pleasant Valley. Here was an abundance of hay, loose or baled, and fodder, corn and oats—all had at low prices that would be haggled over, with wild tossing about of arms and an expert handling of juicy cuss words. We had to bring grain of all kinds, bought from the farmers, into the woods ourselves, and always the purchases were made in winter. For Fred and me, this collaboration with the seasons had two merits: we had a day off from school and, coming home, an opportunity to ride high on a load of sweet-smelling hay.

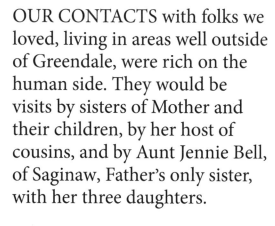

Chapter Twenty-eight

Aunts and Cousins

OUR CONTACTS with folks we loved, living in areas well outside of Greendale, were rich on the human side. They would be visits by sisters of Mother and their children, by her host of cousins, and by Aunt Jennie Bell, of Saginaw, Father's only sister, with her three daughters.

© R.P. Nadeau

LIFE IN A NORTH WOODS LUMBER CAMP

Twenty miles directly south of us was the village of Ithaca, eight miles beyond St. Louis. In and about Ithaca, Mother's parents, with their brothers and sisters, had taken up homesteads in the early forties, hailing from Ohio, where their people, hailing from Pennsylvania and New York State, had homesteaded before them. So it was that in the Ithaca country could be found a Brooke or a Burgess in whatever direction one might turn, each home filled with cousins of Mother's.

These cousins came, sleigh loads of them, in winter, a time when they could get away from their farms and small businesses. They were a gay, lighthearted lot, coming from a world far removed from the lumbering operations of Father and bringing manners and language that in many ways were new to us children. The things that made them hilarious—much of it gay banter—impressed me because they didn't have to go around hitting people on the ear with a snowball or pushing them into the drink in order to be funny.

The cousins' tender worship of Mother and their hearty acceptance of Father endeared them to us and made their coming always an event to be looked forward to. An Irishman was something new in the family, and they adored him—they liked his quick temper, and with it his quick humor, and his stories that always exhibited a world and a kind of life that were new to them. And he on his part was fond of the cousins—he liked them for their laughter and the high spirits they brought.

And then from Saginaw was Father's sister, Aunt Jennie Bell, and her three daughters, from Fred's age on up. Aunt Jennie owned a hotel in Saginaw, and when the girls came to visit us they pitched in and relieved Mother of many duties, ordering the kitchen help around so expertly as to cause them to reach a new height in brisk service.

The Saginaw influence upon my education was entirely musical. Jenny, youngest of the three, mastered the autoharp practically overnight and then showed me how to pick the strings without fairly plucking them out by the roots. She showed me how to play tender airs like "Sweet Afton." The only difficulty was that Afton was not sweet the way I continued playing the air when Jenny had gone home.

It was when Aunt Alma King, Mother's favorite sister, came from Vestaburg with her four children that we O'Donnell youngsters really went places. In descending order Ray, Anna, Celia and Lula almost precisely duplicated our own ages. This paired us off, and although in those early years the infants, Myrtle and Lula, were scarcely aware of how cute they were, and Marie and Celia were busy with their dolls, the older two pairs had weeks each summer of unalloyed fun.

Anna, her mother always said, was a tomboy, which was all right with me. It was from her that I learned the full possibility of smudge pans. Aunt Alma, because of an overdeveloped regard for education, came with her brood only during summer vacations, at a time when in Greendale mosquitoes were at their worst. Evenings, in order to escape the pests, we did not do what might have been expected: stay indoors, barricaded behind

mosquito-netted windows and doors. On the contrary, we went to them, and sat on the back stoop, lured there I suppose by the sun, which looked "real pretty," as Arnie often told us, "a-setting down on the trees over there up Black Crick."

As protection against the swarms of mosquitoes, we sat in a smudge cloud. Our smudge pot was a milk pan that had been discarded as being so old and full of holes that no amount of soldering could help it. Into it we put a layer of sand, covering the bottom. Then we filled it with chips from the woodpile just in front of the woodshed. When the chips were lighted and got going, they were covered over with a fire compost of decayed sawdust, finer chips, and a mixture of sand and other materials found on all well-regulated chip piles. This discouraged the flame and kept the entire business sending out vast volumes of dense smoke. Around this we sat, daring the most eager mosquito to dash in and do his worst.

All of this done, the problem of greater production arose, a problem easily solved by Anna: get more smudge pans, pouring more smoke about and thus discouraging more mosquitoes. We began ransacking the entire camp for more pans, rusting tin pails—we even commandeered Father's tire trough. By dint of the most intense application of our talents, we succeeded in filling them, and when the moment came to initiate the family and guests seated on the stoop, saying how nice the sky looked in the west and how hot the day would be tomorrow, Anna and I burst upon the scene bearing smudge pans from which thick smoke had begun to pour. We had kept our plans secret for surprise effects. We quickly disappeared and as quickly reappeared with others. And again still more smoke rose from the stoop in dark clouds, becoming so thick that Father, only four feet away, called, "Alice, where in thunder are you?"

The two families began coughing from the smoke, each of us edging slowly toward the outer regions of the pall, so that Fred, when Mother wondered what had become of the boys, called out, "I'm over here in Pleasant Valley," and Ray added that he was in Shepherd on his way to Mount Pleasant.

The old lumber "shanty" had limited facilities for comfort.

COURTESY OF DOROTHY PAYTON

It wasn't long before everybody was saying wasn't it about time for bed and, stumbling about in the fog of smoke, each contrived ultimately to reach asylum. Next morning a blue haze hovered above our part of Greendale, with smoke still rising from two or three of our smudge pans.

It was Anna who taught me a new and improved method for catching the green bass that loitered in the deeper places of Potter Creek. "Why fuss around with hooks and lines and worms?" seemed to be her motto.

"You wade through the hole, Tom, and make a lot of noisy noise and I will stand here and catch them when they come upstream!"

This I found was sheer improvisation. It was nothing that Anna had worked out through profound research and practice. The creek in summer was low, in places thinning out over shallow bars so that almost any fish except a green bass or a sucker would, on seeing me, have dived under a log and lain still until danger had passed.

Fred's favorite story... was of Bill McFarren, from over in the Ferris Camp, who one night at the Half Way place came up with six aces. Knives flashed, guns blazed, and when it was all over three men lay stretched out over chairs and table, completely dead.

With a great to-do, thrashing through the water with a branch dropped from a basswood tree, and yelling fit to kill, I beat my way through the hole to where Anna was standing.

The plan worked, but not the way Anna had planned. Approaching her, a bass, around a pound in weight, in order to escape the danger ahead, gave a quick turn to go over a bar and, its plan gone awry, landed on dry ground. Anna was upon it instantly and a new technique had been born. And, demonstrating that the catch was not a fluke, we carried three of them home to our astonished mothers.

Sleeping arrangements, what with eight children in the house, offered a problem that anywhere else would have been insurmountable. This one Fred solved: "Why can't we all sleep on the floor upstairs, all in a row, Ma?" And Mother, Aunt Alma concurring, gave her assent.

The plan worked successfully, chiefly by reason of the vast number of blankets that had been put away for the summer. These, laid on the floor, acres of them, it seemed to us, and several deep, made a bed under the roof that brought early and sound sleep to eight tired children.

Sometimes we three boys, urged on by a desire for greater variety in sleeping arrangements, persuaded Father to put up a tent, and Mother to fill it with blankets. Here the older boys told stories of dark deeds of murder and carnage. Fred always had stored in his mind a few tales of terrible carnage and horror, but Ray one summer struck a new note by telling, with the utmost gruesomeness, about Indian battles being fought in the West. Always when finishing a story, he had a Blackfoot sinking a hatchet deep in the brain of every soldier in the outfit, including the Colonel.

This meant that we would be a long time getting to sleep. Every creak of the tent pole, every cry of a loon from up along the creek, would curdle our blood, including probably Ray's own. For reassurance someone, as he could find voice, would whisper shakingly, "Are you asleep, Fred?"

For the greatest possible variety, we sometimes slept in the haymow. This would always be a social affair on a big scale. Fred would invite all the boys of the neighborhood, thus making it a community event. Having a more considerable setting than a tent, and a large audience on hand, the haymow demanded stories of unusual horror. Fred would start off the occasion with a new story about the Half Way House, his favorite setting for a tale. This grievous spot, where liquor was dispensed and consumed with abandon by its patrons, stood on a high bank of the Chippewa.

Blood-letting in the tales then current was achieved with, variously, guns, fists, and rolling a drunk into the silent waters reflecting an eerie moon a hundred (in the tales) feet below.

Fred's favorite story, which never was told twice alike, and with each new telling was embellished with details of new horrors, was of Bill McFarren, from over in the Ferris Camp, who one night at the Half Way place came up with six aces. Knives flashed, guns blazed, and when it was all over three men lay stretched out over chairs and table, completely dead. "Yes sir, dead as a doorknob, and Bill got away and never has been seen or heard from to this day!"

A new routine featured the events of the night that Ray was with us in the haymow. Flesh-creeping tales had us younger fry completely agog, but even as the program was on we fell asleep, one by one, by the time it was eleven o'clock.

Suddenly, around two o'clock in the morning, Ray, now awake, heard the sounds of a stirring out in the wagon shed. He quickly had Fred awake and the two of them shook in terror as the sounds waxed louder. The whispering soon had the rest of us awake and shaking, my own efforts overtaking my best moments with the ague. By this time we were all wondering what was going on and most of us were whispering in on the discussion.

Suddenly the sound stopped and we were just beginning to think it was Bay Prince maybe kicking against his stall, a favorite pastime of his, when the sounds came again. We soon had it figured out that it was the wagon reach that somebody was trying to steal. I suggested to Ray that he go down and look things over, but he said to go to hell.

Again and again the sounds came, always the sounds followed by a silence more frightening than the sounds. Fred suddenly remembered that Will Jones was not awake and a search for him disclosed that he was not present. A new terror struck our souls. "Well, they got him!" Fred managed to say. "Soon it will be one of us!"

That was it! In my terror I dropped into my "Now I lay me down to sleep" routine when the noises suddenly stopped. I would not need the rest of the prayer, at least tonight. Will suddenly came climbing into the mow, laughing and telling Fred that he ought to have his pa put some oil on that there reach.

Always, when Aunt Alma had taken herself and children home, we waited a decent time, often as long as three weeks, before returning the visit. At such times Father would drive Mother and her brood to Shepherd, there to board a train and set out on a journey of high adventure—"going to Aunt Alma's in Vestaburg!"

In Vestaburg the Greendale routines were repeated, with variations dictated by the fact that in the village were fabulous stores where you bought things on what Ray said was "tick," and twice a day you went over to the depot to see the passenger trains come in and go out. Between times we went over to Bass Lake to swim.

Vestaburg, of course, was not as full as Greendale of exciting people like Pat Moran and Old Man Gibbs, although Uncle Charley did very well. He worked in a shingle mill and when he came home to dinner and supper his clothes were covered all over with fine pine dust that made him, I thought, smell nice. He was as quiet as Father was talkative, the reason being, I was sure, that he was Deputy Sheriff of the County—an office to which in good time he would say good-bye upon being elected Sheriff.

Mrs. Painter, who lived nearby on the corner, was all right too. I never approved completely of the corncob pipe, which she smoked with the bowl upside down, although I approved thoroughly of the gumdrops, which she carried in a pocket and was always handing out to me.

Nor may Peg-leg Joe be omitted from the list of the engrossing personages. Joe really was in the same glamour class with Pat Moran. He was a merry little fellow who, in a careless moment, had lost a leg to a voracious circular saw in the Skidmore sawmill, and who thereby had inspired the song of "Old Dan Tucker"—a detail that I had from Joe himself!

Chapter Twenty-nine

"Bang! Bang!"

© R.P. Nadeau

LIFE IN A
NORTH WOODS
LUMBER CAMP

ON OUR calendar of summer excitements, the Fourth of July sometimes held the A-one spot. At first we spent the day quietly at home, but a year or two later the fame of its lusty celebrations drew us to Shepherd.

Fred and I were the chief participants in our homemade celebrations. By previous arrangement the boys of the neighborhood, to start off the day's program, met soon after breakfast at the swimming hole. On holidays, "after breakfast" was an elastic term. Fred and I, living nearest, would be on hand by eight o'clock. Fred, always marshal for the day, explained to me that his official status put him under bounden duty to be on time and "set a good example to my lieges."

Completely overcome by the grandeur of his language, I felt that I should comment in kind but came within an ace of being unequal to the occasion. Suddenly something out of a story that mother had told me came into my mind and I replied, smartly, "Gadzooks!"

It was not easy being a marshal for any day, let alone the Fourth of July, and having to wait two hours for all of his lieges to show up griped Fred. The first arrival would saunter in around nine o'clock. That usually was Will Jones. Will was for going right in, the three of us, but Fred sternly insisted on waiting for the rest of his subjects. By ten o'clock, however, even Fred could wait no longer, and such as were on hand would shed their duds and plunge into the pool.

One of these years Fred sprang an idea that caught on like—like Jake Wilsey's dog, as he explained to Father at supper. "Jake Wilsey's dog" had reference to a hound that always held particular terror for Fred after an encounter in which he had lost the right leg, most of it, of his pants.

Fred's idea was to make the last boy arriving at the swimming hole "run for it." To run for it meant that the rest of the boys would line up in two rows leading away from the bank of the river. Each boy would be equipped with a handful of wet blue clay with which he would pelt the delinquent as he ran the gauntlet, at the end of the lines plunging into the river.

The idea was adopted with acclaim, and next year every boy had arrived by nine o'clock. This day, unfortunately for the success of the plan, Will Jones was last to arrive and he ran the gauntlet with such skill and speed that he came through unscathed. This achievement meant that next year every kid would want to run the gauntlet. Fate intervened in the person of Joe Hart, who did not arrive until around noon.

Fred, seeing that at this rate we would be spending all day at the swimming hole, moved that the whole idea of the universal running of the gauntlet be dropped. There never was a second to one of Fred's motions, a motion by him being accepted as having been voted upon and the proposal carried unanimously.

By noon on our holidays, we would usually be dressing and turning our backs on the swimming hole, which undoubtedly felt relieved and returned to its normal state, in a quiet spot under big elms that shaded it, and made sweet by the beds of arrowhead and pickerel weed.

The rest of the day's programs would be run off at our home, with activities that began as soon as the kids, or most of them, had returned from their several dinners. Unfortunately for Father, there was really no program at all. Improvisation had a field day. Each boy brought his firecrackers and other fireworks, but that was not enough. No rules governed where torpedoes and such objects would be set off, and Father would no sooner have us out of the woodshed, whose confines emitted an ear-rending roar, than report would reach him that now we were over in the blacksmith shop across Black Creek.

Father would get us out of the blacksmith shop at the cost of a vast amount of heat and, the day being sultry, would be lying on the floor of the sitting room, a copy of the Midland Sun protecting his face from flies, when Mother would come in with tidings that now the boys were down under the wagon shed.

Upon the wagon shed Father would descend, swearing that if it were not for Fred and Tom he would drown the entire—

"Hello, what's this?"

Under the wagon shed Father's eye had lit upon a contrivance that Will had rigged up at home: a bit of gas pipe into which he was pouring a charge of powder. Instantly Father's anger would fall away and he would be all curiosity.

"For God's sake, don't use it that way!"

Will had plugged up what would be the breech end of the pipe with a bit of hickory driven firmly in.

"You will blow your blasted heads off that way. And go up in smoke! Come with me!"

With that he would set out for the blacksmith shop, followed by the entire bunch of boys. At the shop he would discard Will's pipe, finding in our own supply of such things a size to take a cap, which he found in a box of odds and ends. On this he would cut the necessary threads, screw on the cap, and finally drill a touchhole.

"Now," Father would ask, *"what are you going to do with it?"*

*"Fill her full of powder and—bang!"
Will declared, with full dramatic
trimmings.*

*"Yes, and have the blasted thing break
somebody's neck! You must mount it."*

Father, again with the gang in tow, would
take us back to the woodshed, in which were
the remains of an old chipping block cut
from an elm log. On this he would mount
the "gun," binding it with heavy iron straps
and such dinguses as would hold it under
lavish charges of powder.

It is no small trick to get logs on their way once jammed without resorting to dynamite. Generally there was a "key" log that could be moved perhaps only a few feet to start the wood mass moving again, and when that happened, the drivers moved swiftly and surely out of the way. To slip from a log they had been riding, or to fall from a boat from which they operated would have brought a danger which can be appreciated only by those who have seen the tremendous crushing and battering force behind the heavy logs.

COURTESY OF ED KORNMEYER

The howitzer would be a big success, and it was. Not an eyebrow was
so much as singed and Father, walking off the field, a big hero in the eyes
of the boys, was in a state of utter exhaustion.

By six o'clock cannonading would have lost its appeal, and anyhow the
supply of powder, not to mention firecrackers, torpedoes and other items
of terror, would be gone.

"We have to go home for supper anyways," Will would say. *"C'mon, kids!"*

"Ain'tcha coming back?" I was sure to ask.

"Again?" Will asked, and through his nose. He was clearly nauseated by the suggestion. "We been up here twice already today."

And that is how our at-home celebrations went. Fred's and mine, that is, for what with Father still catching up on his sleep after his winter's exhaustions, Mother and Arnie usually busy putting up berries of this and that variety, Pat down along the Salt for shiners, and Marie and Myrtle indifferent to all obligations of patriotism, Fred and I were the only ones left to carry on in the American tradition.

Then came a year when Independence Day took on a wider significance for Fred and me. Father asked if we didn't want to go to Shepherd, where there was to be held a giant celebration. We needed no urging, and when slow-plodding time brought the great day, Father put at our disposal old Mag, the most beloved of our horses next to cream-colored Prince. We were as good as right in Shepherd.

Shepherd was a village of no more than three or four hundred souls, situated on the upper reaches of the Salt. That day, with so grand a program of events, we were thrilled as we entered the village and found a place for Mag in a shed back of the Struble store. In the back end of the buggy were hay and grain for her, and since we removed the buggy and the harness she could indulge her favorite recreation, lying down and dividing the hours between thinking and sleeping.

It was well on into the forenoon when we reached the village, and when we left Mag it was to behold a row of three boweries along Main Street. Already they were filled with dancers, each bowery having two or three sets of dancers going at the same time.

A bowery was essentially a raised platform, struts along the sides supporting light timbers running from corner to corner. Upon these, all along the sides, boughs were placed in such a way as to provide cool walls and a green roof to protect the dancers against the hot sun. At a strategic point in the bowery was the orchestra, consisting of a violin or two, an organ, and sometimes a banjo. The caller, who directed the maneuvers of the square dances (and no others were known) and the collector of the fees completed the personnel.

Around the bowery, along the edges of the platform, was a run a bench made of planks, their ends placed upon blocks sawn from logs and set endwise. Upon these planks was seated a varied assortment of hopeful wallflowers, couples awaiting the next dance, and spectators, mostly people like us, from the farms and backwoods who, filled to the epiglottis with pop, peanuts, popcorn and taffy, thought it a wonderful show that at the same time afforded easement from overheated dogs.

This latter consideration was of special importance to Fred and me. At home our shoes were always put away for the duration in spring, with the consequence that by Independence Day our feet were splayed out in every direction. This, particularly if the day was hot, made the business, not only of getting the shoes on in the first place but of walking around in them, something of an ordeal and a serious handicap to happiness.

Father was a violent devotee of the Congress type of shoe. He had more reasons why people should wear Congress shoes than Congressmen themselves had ever dreamed about. But that was the way with Father— whole-hog devotion to whatever excitement filled him at any given time. Unfortunately, it made little difference what kind of shoe you wore. Any shoe on the hot streets of Shepherd's Fourth of July would have the wearer on the ropes by mid-afternoon.

As we sat in a bowery I nudged Fred and told him my feet were busting and he told me to take off my shoes then. This I did, but immediately regretted the act, for hot, shooting flames began to run through my feet and halfway to my knee.

We sat through seven sets of dances, and Fred then said how about going and getting some pop. This I was for, but when I tried to put on my shoes the feet rebelled so that the rest of the day I had to go barefoot, completely unembarrassed as I carried my footgear, stockings and elastics tucked inside the shoes, under my arm.

Outside of the boweries new notes and gaiety were furnished by the "stands"—concessions strung along the sidewalks where pop, lemonade, taffy, peanuts, firecrackers and such were called to our attention by glib vendors who told one and all to "come up, ladies and gents! Come up, run up, any way to get up. Ice-cold lemonade five cents a glass!" Any and all wares were sold with similar compelling calls.

To two boys from the hinterland, it was all a bewildering array of good things to eat and drink. It was so bewildering that although the dollar you were given to spend was burning holes in your pocket, you would go up and down the street an hour before you could decide upon a sack of peanuts and, maybe, a bottle of pop.

> **...concessions strung along the sidewalks where pop, lemonade, taffy, peanuts, firecrackers and such were called to our attention by glib vendors who told one and all to "Come up, ladies and gents! Come up, run up, any way to get up. Ice-cold lemonade five cents a glass!**

The family long cherished a story of Marie's first visit to a celebration. Torn between the appeals made by the lemonade, pop, taffy, and long, thin strips of coconut candy, she spied bunches of tender young wintergreen shoots, priced at five cents a bunch. To make a plunge into spending, she blew her first dime for two bunches, one for herself and one for Myrtle—and with acres of fresh, young wintergreen across Black Creek that we never thought of eating.

At the main four corners of the village, a platform for the orator of the day had been erected. By one o'clock the crowd would be gathering, all agog at the prospect of seeing a real live State Senator, the Hon. Jabez A. Bickthorn, or somebody, from Gladwin. Precisely at 2:20, although the handbills said he would take off at 2:00 sharp, the honorable gentleman ascended the platform, looked up to the top of the pole where the Stars and Stripes hung limp in the heat, cleared his throat, took from his pocket a gold, hunting-case watch and solemnly checked on the sun, drew a handkerchief from the tail of his Prince Albert coat and waited for the dignitaries to get seated without their chairs slipping off the edge of the platform and breaking their necks.

At last all was ready: The last acquaintance was waved to by Arch Strobe, and Will Dent, the chairman of the day, would get up and give the life story of the Honorable Jabez. The audience, duly spellbound by Will's oratory, went wild when the speaker of the day finally was on his feet and reminded the audience that today we celebrate the birthday of our great country. He ended an hour later, with his left hand over his heart and the right one pointing to the flag still hanging limp at the tip of the pole.

It was a grand occasion, almost as grand as the times when Father, if pressed, would recite Bobby Burns's "MacPherson's Farewell," which for my money was the height of rhetorical effort. The speech made me almost glad that my feet hurt because they felt so good when, roused by the speaker's stirring phrases, I momentarily forgot my foot troubles.

All day long, as a kind of backdrop for the occasion, was the never-ending sidewalk parade. Up and down both sides of Main Street people, having just been to Struble's store, were now going down to Dent's store for something else. Boys weaving along the walk whistled to trios of girls arm-in-arm just ahead of them. The Joneses and the Browns and the Averys from over our way sat perilously on the hitching rails, jawing about old times.

Toward evening, you were aware of a note of expectancy in the air. As soon as it was dark enough there would be fireworks. This was an eerie business. In the growing darkness you could discern figures assembling on the roof of the barbershop, carrying things and arranging equipment for the glories to come. Suddenly the hammering and shouting would cease and after a breathless pause you heard a loud noise that told you just one thing: A Roman candle was opening the show.

When the crowd had recovered from the swu-ush of the candle, and the beauty of the cascade of red, green and yellow balls of light, you were ready for everything that followed. The sky rocket, the pinwheels, the red powder that rose, billowing clouds of red smoke, the red, white and blue paper balloons that went up and up, carried by such breezes as now stirred and disappearing over in the direction of the clothespin factory, the show at an end when men began climbing down from the roof of the barber shop.

What a day, what a day! It was lucky that old Mag, once put on the road home, needed no driver. Barely had we turned off Main Street onto the road to Greendale than Fred and I were fast asleep, living it all over in our dreams. I did not remember reaching home or going to bed.

The next day we would devote to a recap of our day in Shepherd, reminding each other of the things we had neglected to see, like the ballgame at Salt River, a village that adjoined Shepherd on the east, and the blasts of powder placed under anvils that were set off by Will Harmon, the blacksmith. These things we vowed we would see next year.

Chapter Thirty

Woods Afire

TERROR STRUCK the hearts of the family one hot August day along toward the end of our lumbering operations. For days the sky had been hazy—a kind of haze that told too clearly of smoke from fires in the forests to the north of us. Word had come in of extensive fires in Clare and Gladwin counties.

The Chippewa River, with its broad river bottoms and intervals of burned-over land along its north shore, formed what Father considered a considerable barrier against fires trying to reach across into our area of Greendale.

Suddenly a new sultriness was in the air. More and more, the haze assumed a definite character of smoke, and in a few hours the air had the undeniable smell of fire. The flames were on their way! And then one night in the sky appeared a faint glow that slowly, but surely, grew brighter by the hour.

All of our settlers, Alex Jones, Jake Wilsey, and the others to the south of us were in comparative safety, ours being the last family as one went into the woods. More and more men began to show up in order to discuss the situation with Father.

Danger lay chiefly in the triangle described by a line running from our home westward

© R.P. Nadeau

LIFE IN A NORTH WOODS LUMBER CAMP

to Mount Pleasant, then down the Chippewa to a point due north of us, and, turning south, to arrive at our settlement. In the region so described were a few sections of uncut timber, which for reasons of their own the owners were not cutting or putting on the market. Our own timber by now was nearly gone, and in any case did not lie in the path of the fire. The problem for us would be to keep the flames from crossing Black Creek. Should the fire leap across the stream and destroy our camp, it could continue on to the homes of the families to the south of us.

At last came an hour when we could hear, through the choking smoke, sounds of the fire as the flames swept relentlessly on, the clouds of smoke billowing above the fire and glowing red even in the daylight.

The situation, so far as it affected our personal safety, was not of epic quality. We could escape, but our camp must be saved. Fires in the counties to the north of us had laid waste scores of square miles of virgin timber and taken their share of lives, and destroyed untold amounts of wild game. The clearing of a considerable amount of land to the south would reduce the costs of a fire, but the families had only the most meager resources, wherefore for every reason it was necessary to stop the fire at Black Creek.

The danger, all could see, was chiefly from embers and flaming debris that might be carried by the winds across the creek. From the creek to the fringe of timber was perhaps a hundred yards. On our side of the stream, the house was a third of that distance from the creek. The house and shanties and buildings in the barnyard offered an acre of hot, dry roofs, quick food for stray sparks and live coals.

Here was our first job: to protect all our buildings against sparks and hot debris carried by the wind across the creek. This much done, we would just have to let nature take its course.

Father called for water, barrels of it, to be brought from the spring and brook. The spring, of blessed memory, was at the foot of the hill. In the muck of the low ground, two barrels, bottoms removed, had been sunk.

Above the overflow from the barrels Father, when we became keepers of cows, had built a milk shed. Here on shelves Mother kept rows of brown earthenware crocks of milk, arranged neatly by days and milking time, whether morning or night. Within the shed Father had sunk a half-barrel to receive the overflow of water from above. In this Mother kept butter and Dutch cheese in tall crocks.

The atmosphere within the shed made it the coolest place anywhere about in the hot days and nights of summer. And also the sweetest place, if you liked to go around smelling things. Here was the smell of milk and butter, and from all around one caught the smell of lush growths of plants native to low places, particularly like the red and blue lobelia, the closed gentian, the touch-me-not, and several members of the mint family. The touch-me-not, next to Dutchman's breeches and lady slippers, was the number one flower with us younger children. Down by the spring we spent hours hovering over the bright green plants, exploding between thumb and finger the fat, ripe seedpods, seeing seeds fly off in every direction to rattle softly through the plants as they fell to the ground.

Today nobody was thinking about touch-me-nots, as near a dozen men dashed down the hill and hurried back with pails filled with water, emptied them into barrels and other receptacles, and dashed down again and again for more water.

Other men were on the ladder-climbing detail. Up ladders they hurried, to spread blankets over the roofs and wet them down with water. The heat, of course, dried out the blankets in short time, a fact that kept the labors of the ladder men as continuous as those of the water carriers.

All of these activities started none too soon, for presently the fire had reached the rim of trees beyond Black Creek. The heat from the fire fairly seared our faces and hands, and the crackling of the flames and the crashing to the ground of burned-off branches, and even entire trees, added to the terror that shook me, as it probably did all of us, to the foundation.

This was my first and only forest fire, so I cannot check on previous or later experiences, but in my mind the sensations that stood out with extreme vividness were the livid shades of each burning trunk or branch, even the smallest, as they were limned, pink, against the hot sky.

Lumberjacks were all capable of doing any part of the work or taking over any particular job when necessary, and they did it with pride.

Throughout the day the drama continued; all day the hot and begrimed crew of men watched for flying sparks and kept blankets soaked with water. Dozens of fires got going in dry grass about the premises. Let a wisp of smoke appear, however, and a man suddenly was there with water in a pail. Sparks dropped perilously close to buildings, and frequently on the front stoop, and again on the woodshed roof, but a dash of water from a ready pail and they were out.

Mother and Arnie had not been less busy than the men. These were hungry men, and well before noon they began to come into the house in shifts of twos and threes. This, it may be added, was the day (second in the family's list of dramatic highlights only to the time Fred slugged it out with a skunk, which, thinking it a woodchuck, he wanted to bring home alive) when I was so absorbed with my work that I went all day until supper without food.

At last, well on toward darkness, there seemed to be a feeling in the mind of everyone that the danger had passed. The roar of the flames had lessened ever so slightly and the heat seemed less intense.

Undoubtedly the fire had been letting itself down for some time. No one, however, relaxed his vigilance until Father said, confidently, that the fury was licked and now let's take it easy. No one needed urging. Again Arnie came out with a pail of tea. The men drank dippersful, and then, in reaction to the excitements of battle, began to sit down on the back stoop or lie stretched out on the ground—anywhere in their weariness, so long as they didn't have ever to walk again.

An hour later the danger was quite over, and now a grand supper was to be served for all hands. A perfect ending to a day of alarms, as this one had been.

Next day an investigation made clear that the fire had kept veering to the west sufficiently to save Father's holdings of timber, making the happiness of our family complete.

Chapter Thirty-one

Old John Whitesell

YEAR BY YEAR, as the pine and hemlock disappeared under Father's efforts, a kind of clean-up business of one kind or another would get under way. It had started when Jake Wilsey came in with his mill and found considerable timber for his saws in the form of second-grade pine and hemlock, and even of long-butts of trees that had been left on the ground by our sawyers.

The manner in which great trees were butted would later on have brought tears to the eyes of conservationists, men who even then were beginning to be heard from, although in Greendale without ardent enthusiasm.

A felled tree would first be examined to ascertain whether it was "shaky"—meaning whether the heart of it was sound at the base. If it was sound, good. If, on the other hand, shakes or other evil signs were present, the eye of the sawyers discovered how far up the tree the shakes extended—five feet, ten feet, or even more. The tree would then be "short-butted" or "long-butted," loose terms that too often would include in the butt sound timber that should have gone to Saginaw, rather than be left on the ground to rot away.

© R.P. Nadeau

LIFE IN A NORTH WOODS LUMBER CAMP

Butts, the longer of them, now began to come to Jake's mill for sawing into lumber. There would be a good deal of waste, yet a considerable amount of timber was thus salvaged.

Besides material of this kind, there was timber furnished by the woods that grew along the river flats, among these beautiful trees the tall butternuts, which, with curly maple and cherry, was sawn into lumber for the Grand Rapids furniture factories. Almost anything, for that matter, was used for lumber, since as fast as the timber was cut away, settlers were coming in and the frail houses which they ran up could be made from ash or any other timber for all they cared.

> **So it was now, Joe turned on me and said that if I didn't get the hell out of there he'd throw me in the creek. I went, having made unusual progress for one day. Promptly I would be back the next morning, instinct directing me to the one spot where my talents would be most destructive of morale.**

Jake was just beginning to feel that his business was on the way when suddenly a shingle mill was set up on the bank of the Salt, back a quarter of a mile from what had been the Green place. The owner and operator of the mill was a son of Father's by a former marriage. Recently he had run a successful mill in Shepherd. He was the jolliest of the O'Donnell clan, and with him were two children to join our group: Fred, two years younger than our Fred (who thus became known as "Little Fred") and Jennie, of near my own age.

From the start, Joe must have wondered why the good fates that thus far had kept me out of his life should now have brought him headlong into my midst. Before the mill was completed, and while he was busy directing the details of putting the bolter here and a knot-saw there, and over yonder the packing bins, I was on hand, learning the business from the ground up.

"What is a planer, Joe?"

"Planer? Let's see—why, a planer is a, a planer."

"Oh!"

Having got this information digested, I contemplated another machine and after a spell of deep thinking I asked about it.

"What's that, Joe? That thing there."

"That? Why, that is the shingle machine and it saws the shingles."

"What's that dingus there?" and I pointed to the upper part of the machine under our discussion.

"That?" Resisting an impulse to smack me, he went on, "That is the carriage. You put the shingle bolts on it and shove them back and forth over the saw, and shingles come out."

"When?"

This latter question, of the why-when-where type, was the way I always handled such problems, although calculated to bring a discussion to an abrupt end. So it was now. Joe turned on me and said that if I didn't get the hell out of there he'd throw me in the creek. I went, having made unusual progress for one day. Promptly I would be back the next morning, instinct directing me to the one spot where my talents would be most destructive of morale.

My enthusiasm for the shingle business was by this time boundless, and if my particular form of asking questions failed to draw forth much information, yet I learned a good deal by looking on from a perch on a convenient stump or a stack of shingles. Thus it was that soon I was doing jobs like laying shingles in the packing frames. Later on I would be completing my education in that department by pulling down the long lever to the ground and standing on it as I took nails from my mouth and drove them home, one by one, through the thin iron strap that would hold the shingles tight at the middle of the bunch. It was a long time, however, before I was permitted to do more than look at a saw. Mother said I didn't have too many fingers anyhow, and Joe told me to keep away from anything that had teeth in it.

Thus it was early that I made up my mind that shingle weaving was my dish. The smell of the sawdust, the curl of the thin shavings as they came from the planer, the merry yip-yip of the knot-saw, a baby affair that from a shingle cut away any part containing a knot—and above all the way the shingle weaver wore his pants!

This latter touch of gentility had all of the qualities of a grand art. Next to his "reddies," the weaver wore a pair of stunning trousers, usually of a dark gray or blue, and showing through, a cunningly devised stripe. It was always the stripe that got you. Joe's pants were of the conventional shingle-weaver type, with a dark red silk thread running through the stripe pattern, producing an effect upon which I would spend hours in ecstatic contemplation. Over his pants the fastidious maker of shingles wore his blue overalls, the legs rolled neatly to just below the knee, displaying the lower part of each trouser leg to the admiring gaze of a ravished public.

Then there was old John Whitesell, who as a pioneer operator belongs in this recital. John had been in the region long before we arrived, carrying on a one-man business. His work was in timber, however, albeit alone, removed from other men, and he possessed a character that would grace the pages of a book of gold.

Fred undoubtedly had heard of John, but in any case we came across him one day, north from our camp toward the Chippewa River, at the edge of a black-ash swale, a mile, two miles, from his camp. Here, sitting astride a shaving bench with a drawshave, making barrel hoops, we first saw him. As a matter of fact, we saw him but a time or two thereafter, for a year or two later he returned to his native "York State."

It is possible that John came originally to Greendale with the Gibbses, drawn to these frontiers in part by a desire to escape from some secret hurt, and in part by a nature that to start with had leanings in the direction of

solitude. He had built a shanty within sight of the Chippewa, and there he lived alone, picking and selling berries in summer, making hoops, fishing a little and in winter setting traps for otter, muskrats and such other fur-bearing animals as he found a ready market for in Mount Pleasant. His wants were few and he seemed to be content with the scanty income his activities provided.

Construction of the O'Donnell's lumber settlement could not begin before timber was taken off the forested area.

In appearance John was not unlike John Burroughs, beard and all. His manner was gentler than was the great naturalist's. He talked little enough, but if he did not give you a great deal of his history, between the wide-spaced lines there was much that you could read. He directed his conversation to Fred, and it speaks volumes for the strength of his personality that never did my dander rise at his clear neglect of me.

"I like these swales," he told Fred. "I've never seen their like anywhere else. I suppose there is some reason why they are like that just here. But you could say the same thing about me, and about you, and I don't ask questions about that either. I can work in the sun all day and hear the wind in the trees, and talk with the birds—for they come right up to where you are sitting and talk, kind of, and then after sizing me up awhile they will fly into a tree and sing for me."

In Fred John had a sympathetic audience, even if, as I suspect, he didn't understand too much of what the old man was saying. Both of us listened intently, so much so that he was encouraged to go on.

"Maybe you've noticed these swales, when the leaves have gone—how blue they are with the sunlight on them. In winter with the snow they are even more wonderful. I come here to this one, which is the finest of them all, a good deal in the winter."

I thought Fred had put his foot in it when he asked why, if he liked swales so much, he cut down the black ashes in them for his barrel hoops. John was ready with an answer. He pointed to a pile of hoops beside him, and then to the stack of poles ready to be shaved.

"Can you see," and he pointed to the swale, "where I took these trees from?"

Fred couldn't, and John continued.

"I take them out of just here and there like. Not enough from any one place to be missed. They are the bigger ones and they would be dying any time now. By taking them out I make room for the young ones to grow up and take their places."

John talked about that and other things like it that day, and in a quiet voice that seemed a very part of the setting. He was an unforgettable figure whose influence upon people who came in contact with him must have been such that when at last he was taken, others had been fashioned in his spirit to take his place in the swale that he would have called Life.

THE "SOLDIERS' REUNION," to be held that year at Mount Pleasant, for Fred and me was in the same category as Fourth of July celebrations. For Pat Moran it would eclipse this year in grandeur, and by far overshadow the annual doings at Shepherd.

Chapter Thirty-two

Pat and His pals

At the Reunion you had a huge parade, many minor ones of individual outfits, veterans in Grand Army of the Republic uniforms, and brass bands and fife and drum corps all over the blasted place, as Fred afterward described the affair to Will Jones.

At night, as Fred went on, there was a sham battle, filling the sky with bombs bursting here and there in the air, big guns booming and shells screaming all over the sky. What I missed, of course, were the oceans of pop so popular in Shepherd at Fourth of July celebrations.

I could easily have stayed at home, but when word reached us of the impending doings I was the first to announce a determination to attend. Fred viewed the idea without enthusiasm, but gave in when Father suggested that Pat, as a matter of fact, could not be trusted out of our sight.

So it was that Fred and I set out for the official seat of Isabella County, Pat having

© R.P. Nadeau

LIFE IN A NORTH WOODS LUMBER CAMP

already gone. For Pat there would be old friends to drink with and to haggle with over the merits of respective outfits. He walked the distance to Mount Pleasant, as did we.

Fred and I reached the village around noon and were ecstatic as we looked upon the flags and bunting all over the place. With a casual, man-of-the-world air, Fred wondered where we could find dinner, both of us tuckered out after our long hike. Presently we were in front of a restaurant. Fred knew, I could see, all about restaurants, whereas this, if we entered, would be my first intro-duction to places where you actually paid money for the privilege of eating.

> The climax of the day's excitements came with the sham battle at night. The hell-fire and fury of this you took mostly on faith. The night was dark enough to obscure most of the action and you wondered how men taking part in the opposing armies were not half the time butchering their own men.

We entered, and presently Fred was dis-posing of a steak, surrounded by potatoes and such. For myself, I was too flabber-gasted, as Fred read off the list of dishes, to make a choice and settled for what ended up being three pieces of huckleberry pie and a glass of milk. Each of us flaunted what we were sure was the air of a man of the world, although none of the other diners seemed impressed by the sang-froid with which we ordered and consumed our food.

Increased activity in the street soon had our attention, and our last bite was scarcely stowed away when a Zouave band from Detroit marched past, filling the air with "Tenting on the Old Camp Ground."

The big parade of the day was to start at two o'clock, and by one-thirty Fred and I had piled into the back seat of a surrey standing beside a har-ness store. We had promised Pat to be on the lookout for him, and when the march got under way, Post after Post going by in uniform, flags and banners flying and bands blaring, we were without sign of the old warrior. We feared for the worst as Fred reminded me of Pat's drinking capacities.

Our fears were in vain, for presently Pat's Post appeared, every man stepping smartly to music, and behind it, a full hundred feet, Pat, alone with his best limp, his cane thump-thumping the ground and face set straight ahead, every bit the Moran of Greendale. In spite of his rather casual endeavor, the parade gained on the distinguished hero of Cold Spring, and by the time he reached the disbanding point his group was over at a tent having a drink. Afterward, Pat explained to me that he always was put at the end of a parade. It was his favorite spot, he told me, since then you could take your own time.

Pat in his post-parade activities was an undoubted success. The day was hot and we were always running into him, toasting a host from somebody's bottle and making up for the months of abstemious living in our camp.

The climax of the day's excitements came with the sham battle at night. The hell-fire and fury of this you took mostly on faith. The night was dark enough to obscure most of the action and you wondered how men taking part in the opposing armies were not half the time butchering their own men.

One line of action held you spellbound: the shells that kept lobbing all over the sky and bursting just like you sang about in the "Star Spangled Banner." The din of it was beautiful and you wished you could take some of it home with you for Pa and Ma to see and hear. Pat of course was out there somewhere, being complimented by a Colonel, at least a Colonel, upon the way he led that charge over the worm fence back of the grist mill, where the Chippewa flowed past. Pat, being a big gun like this, made you feel in a way that this was really your own private battle.

The struggle on the field was at last over, won by Pat's army. This fact we had from Pat later on, back in Greendale where there would be no one to dispute the claim. The action on the field took more out of Fred and me than it did the veterans, and soon we were looking for a place to sleep. Fred said let's go and find somewhere to stay. Every place, of course, was long ago taken and we decided upon a haystack, if we could find space not already pre-empted. Luck was with us, for what we found was a straw-stack, so vastly better for our purposes than a haystack. Others were ahead of us, but we found a space that was unoccupied and here, after excavating with our hands a capacious cave, we lay down, feet first, soon fast asleep.

Toes and fingers intact next morning, we repaired to our restaurant;

Work horses were indispensable
in hauling out timber.
COURTESY OF *THE INDEPENDENCE*

then, bent on going home, we went in search of Pat, who would be gleeful at the good tidings. He would be staying on to the end of the festivities. Eventually we found him, bottle in hand and about to drink a toast to a veteran from St. Louis. We imparted to him our tidings, and he bore the news with an aplomb that we felt was a credit to his eminence in the Grand Army of the Republic.

We found no lift home, but the long walk seemed really short by reason of Fred's analysis of the battle of the night before. As he told it I could see that, although nothing was at stake, for sheer strategy and tactics the struggle would occupy in history a place alongside the struggles at Austerlitz and Blenheim.

The expedition to Mount Pleasant increased Fred's and my reputations as military authorities among the boys of our neighborhood. We placed ourselves unreservedly at the service of our public, and a kid displayed indifference to our manifestos at imminent peril of having an eye or two neatly blacked. In our expositions we added such details as would heighten interest in the minds of our public. On one occasion Fred hinted darkly that Pat was far more than what he passed himself off as being—that maybe, if the truth were known, he was a Major General in disguise.

Within the past year Pat had begun to talk wistfully to Fred and me about the Soldiers' Home at Grand Rapids. Several of his old cronies were there now, and at Mount Pleasant he had dwelt with enthusiasm upon the glories of life with fellow comrades. Father, through Fred and me, had learned of all this and was going to urge Pat to take the step if he desired. Pat made his own decision, and in favor of retirement, and at once. Pronto like!

His decision thus acted upon by proper officials, Pat set off on a journey that would take him to scores of friends and to restful days that Greendale could not give him. He went with our good wishes and affection.

Chapter Thirty-three

The Last Drive

OLD PAT'S EXIT from the Greendale stage was but one of a series of changes that soon led to our final curtain. The first of the changes came upon the end of our last drive.

The drive, or "river drive," as in Greendale at least it was so called, was always the thrilling climax to a season's lumbering operation. Soon after the return to camp of the men in autumn, a daily routine would have been fallen into. At five o'clock in the morning, sleepy-eyed men would sit down to breakfast, then climb onto the sleighs for a ride to the cutting operations; a ride to camp for dinner at noon and the ride back again; supper at six, and then a couple of hours when saws would be filed and set, axes ground, patches put here and there on pants and shirts, a turn at double pedro or another game with well-worn decks of cards, maybe an attempt at singing a shanty song or two, and at last to bed.

It was all very routine and uneventful, until along in March you sensed a quickening of the collective pulse. You were aware suddenly of lengthening days and were not surprised when some of the men got out their river boots, gave them a thorough greasing and looked to broken and missing calks from the rigors of the previous drive.

© R.P. Nadeau

LIFE IN A NORTH WOODS LUMBER CAMP

Then one day the scaler showed up and started work on the rollways. The break-up of winter was not far away, and sure enough a warm drizzling rain stole in one night, and by mid-forenoon or noon the sleighs were unable to get their loads to the banking ground because of the large bare spots on the road. Father, after scanning the sky and sniffing the air, called off all work except that of breaking the rollways and getting all logs into the water, already close to bank full.

Presently other men, armed with peavies, began to show up at the camp, river drivers hired by Father to supplement those of our regular force who would take part in the drive. Already above the rollway the water was backed up far above the tiers of logs extending even beyond the opposite bank.

Thus it was that with the ice breaking up into huge cakes and on the down-river side of the rollways the stream bank full, the men went to work breaking the rollways. Loosen a few key logs toward the bottom of a rollway, and whole sections would follow and, in loose water, would go floating away with little further help except direction by men stationed along the river with peavies or pike poles. The lowest tier broken, the next tier above it would be tackled, and so on to the last tier on the banking ground.

No sooner had the first logs started down the river than men followed to take up positions at points where there was danger of jams forming. Logs must always be kept in the stream to prevent jamming and to make sure that logs did not at low spots float out over the banks and become stranded on the flats.

The river driver's conveyance in getting about was always a log, which with pike pole or peavey he mounted, riding with ease and skill to the spot below that threatened to become the site of a jam. If a jam was already under way, it would be his job to find the key log and, freeing it, get the entire stretch of backed-up logs moving again.

In the meantime, a wide, stout raft was being made by hitching as many as five or six logs, long ones, together. This would be commissary and general headquarters, and would carry dishes and cooking utensils, blankets and the men's turkeys. There would be precious little time for sleep, for a jam was no respecter of persons or hours.

From the first, Father had permitted Fred to go along on the drives—as Admiral of the Rafts, Fred always put it. At the age of fifteen, he had become an expert rider of logs, and insisted that he take his place with the men. Father not only gave in, but let me have the post left vacant by Fred. In this office, I was, first, to keep myself from always being under-foot and, second, as occasion might seem to demand, to seize a pike pole and ease the raft away from banks and into the current of the river.

In good time the last log was got into the Chippewa. We said our good-byes to the men and Father, Fred and I, in a wagon which Alex Jones had driven down for the purpose, stowed our equipment and started for home.

Our final drive followed the pattern of the former ones except that as the men left the river to hit the road that would take them to Midland, there were quavers in the voices of men who had been regulars in our operations.

Changes now in our activities were marked. So long as timber remained, we would carry on. This remaining timber was of two kinds: the small stands of pine and hemlock back in the woods, and on the river flats a considerable quantity of hardwood, chiefly elm and basswood. The pine and hemlock would be sawn into lumber by Jake Wilsey, and into shingles by Joe's mill. The hardwood would be sawn by us into bolts—elm bolts for the stave mills at St. Louis, and basswood bolts for the clothespin plant in Shepherd.

To the most casual observer, the timber could not last beyond a year or two. The pine and hemlock were all but gone, and in the place of the majestic trees there grew up areas covered with small, useless, low-growing plants like the wild cherry, poplar, and berry bushes of several kinds, all mixed in with debris of limbs and tops and butts of trees which we had cut down. Such areas presented a ghastly sight, but fortunately it was seldom necessary to go among them.

A considerable number of families were talking of moving out. Two or three had already gone, and later when we did move, only one family remained, the people who had bought our home. All had given up hope of deriving a living from the light soil. What once had been a veritable Eden for two young lads had now, bereft of its timber, become a sorry symbol of infertility.

And came a day when, the last bolts loaded on sleighs, Fred cracked a whip and was off with them to Shepherd. The family turned to arrangements for removal to a more likely scene, out in the Pine River country, and within the month, in a blinding snowstorm, we set out, on our Last Drive!

THERE WERE MOVING
reminders of the past in the
remains of an old logging dam
on the Chippewa River where
the road from Shepherd inter-
sects the road to Midland.
A short distance west, on the
south side of the Big Salt River's
former banking grounds, were
rusting relics and bits of a lumber
camp ruins north of Greendale,
where neglected overgrown
fields, collapsing stone walls and
decaying stumps of monumental
softwoods hint that once a settlement existed there.

There was little to suggest of the old home-
place, but for the four observant siblings the
thin soil, an iron horseshoe, the metal rim
from a wooden wagon wheel, stone foundations and neglected, very old fruit trees told
a meaningful story: their history.

A half-century after the family left Greendale, when Tom and Fred O'Donnell and their
sisters returned to the site of O'Donnell Lumber Camp, they found more open land than
what had once been there. Black, Onion and
Potter Creeks and Spring Brook, from which
many buckets of water had been toted home,
were still flowing freely. There was even a

Place of Dreams

© R.P. Nadeau

LIFE IN A
NORTH WOODS
LUMBER CAMP

mound of decomposed logs that denoted the location of the camp's log school, and depressions in the earth indicated where homes in the later years of the camp once stood.

The unseen things that remained for Tom and his siblings were all those struggles for survival, the overpowering tiredness of the lumberjacks, the forest through which the children journeyed, and the mother and father they would never again in this world see. The long dirt roads that led to the nearby cities where the O'Donnell kids learned about life apart from the logging woods were connections that reminded them of old friends and youthful days.

During all those long-ago years of their youth, they hadn't given a thought to what sorts of childhoods they were living. Only then, as a grandfather himself, did a flood of stories inundate Tom's mind as family legend. So Tom decided to write of the days when he and his siblings were growing up. His youth must have seemed a golden age, even though it would not have been for his parents. There were hurdles in the 1880s and 1890s that brought many a family to their knees.

"I don't know much about Grandpa's early life," Grandson Tom said many years later. At seventy-seven years old, he now wishes he had been more attentive when he "rode around the back roads with his writer-grandfather. "I was ten years old when Grandpa decided to begin locating old-timers around Boonville. He'd take me on interviews." Grandfather and grandson would talk with old guides like Del Belinger, locate the grave of famed hunter-trapper Nat Foster, and listen to former lumberjacks and railroad men.

Young Tom learned about "floating," a practice long outlawed, and the ingenious ways the early poachers used to beat the law. They heard about an unorthodox character, "Kettle" Jones, and how his pet raccoon dunked its food in Kettle's home-made brandy as the pair ate together. Grandfather and grandson listened to Pony Bob tell of his horse-trading days and traveled to old communities no longer on the maps. "You don't want to miss the story of the jack who went over Niagara Falls riding his log," a famed local figure would say." Nevertheless, young Tom recalled, "I remember I was bored, bored to death. The roads were rough back then and the men would talk on" for hours, it seemed. "One thing I have always remembered because I thought it unusual was Grandpa never attended the same church. Every Sunday he would go somewhere different. One week he'd go to a Methodist service, then attend a Catholic church. Another Sunday he'd go to a Baptist church, then a Presbyterian, and so forth.

"I also remember hearing stories of how Grandpa's folks had struck it rich logging in the Maine woods, but had somehow lost it all by the time they established their Michigan camp."

O'Donnell was not an Adirondack "old-timer" in the narrow sense. For more than 20 years, he made a habit of spending his summers near Boonville, New York. "In 1937," Tom A. O'Donnell said, "it was my grandfather who had learned that the *Boonville Herald* was looking for an editor. Walter D. Edmunds, the well-known author [of *Rome Haul* and *Drums Along the Mohawk*, was a close friend. He summered at his parent's home." The farm, called Northlands, was along the Black River in Hawkinsville. "I assume he learned about the position from him, just like he'd learned about the North Country from Edmunds. He told my father about it."

The little northern town and its people reminded Thomas C. of his past. It suited him, and when he retired in 1946 as production manager for the Robert M. McBride Publishing Company in New York City, it was to Boonville that he came to settle down for an active period of writing and research.

The Adirondacks and their foothills, the neighboring towns of Forestport and Woodgate, the cities of Rome and Utica—all these furnished the themes for the books he wrote.

O'Donnell told a newspaper man who was covering the author's latest book about Fairfield Seminary that he had a keen interest in sectional history and that he had written "eight to ten other books" before he got started on his current [north country] series. One was a gardening book, *A Garden for You*, "which attracted much attention among plant growers." Prior to his "publishing house position, he was for 16 years editor of the New York Masonic Outlook," the unnamed columnist for the Herkimer *Evening Telegraph*, told.

By the late 1940s Thomas C. O'Donnell's time and study were chiefly devoted to talking with old timers—such as the colorful preacher-collector of Adirondack history, Rev. A. L. Byron-Curtiss of North Lake—and others who remembered some of the events and figures of more than half a century back. He also spent a good deal of time going over old newspapers, books and records. His collection of material is stored in volumes of cartons which are anything but drab statistical summaries and are touched with keen appreciation for the days when the edges of the Adirondacks were dotted with centers of industry and trade.

O'Donnell relished the stories of early engineers, the founding of the Bisby Club and the famed Adirondack League Club, and the sawmill era with its famed lumberjacks. Tales of the old communities no longer on the map, Farrtown and Wheelertown, of Pony Bob's, Reed's Mill and Enos enlivened his imagination.

Clearly, judges in and around Forestport that gave the game protectors a bad time, the notorious Dirty Dozen who took vengeance on game wardens assigned to patrol the Adirondack League Club land, Forestport's Liars Club and "The Harness Shop Senate," which held its meetings in Sam Utley's harness shop in Forestport, provided much hilarious material for O'Donnell's facile pen. The guides too were colorful.

Grandfathers and grandmothers, uncles and aunts, Civil War veterans, aged farmers, loggers, merchants, local historians, and postmasters all were great storytellers and were delighted to talk of earlier times.

O'Donnell knew the modern age was on the horizon and he, the author of numerous books, knew he too straddled the generations and had absorbed much from each. While he lived in Chicago, he was involved with numerous "little" magazines, often the first venue of unknown writers. O'Donnell contributed to these magazines, and also helped to foster what might be called a truly American type of literature. He was friendly with all of the young poets who were part of the Harriet Monroe "Poetry" group, and his book shelves were lined with autographed copies of their books.

In 1902, O'Donnell left America to finish his studies in England. In London, he met and married his wife Bertha in 1905. The Irish poets Padraic Colum, Shaemus O'Sheel and James Stephens were intimate friends of the O'Donnells, and were frequent visitors to the O'Donnell home.

But while his professional life was a worldly-wise one, and his social contacts well-known writers, his Salt River recollections remained fond ones.

The old lumber camp was a perfect place for day-dreaming and care-free times, for clean fun with childhood friends, and for being looked after and well-nurtured by caring parents who taught the children about responsibility by enlisting them to do whatever jobs fit their capabilities.

"I was aged in wood," was an expression Tom used when comparing his boyhood experiences and living conditions with those of his grandson's youth.

The physical work and the change of the seasons presented challenges. Each family member was required to pitch in to prepare for winter. Raising a limited amount of livestock along with a portion of their produce required teamwork. The O'Donnell children's assistance was required to help stack hay in mounds, store ears of corn in rodent-proof cribs, tend to chickens and the care of the hen house, assist in canning and pickling, filling the root cellar, smoking meat, fetching water, splitting stove wood for the kitchen range, and so many other necessary chores. In those days, all family responsibilities came before playtime.

These are flights of the imagination—but not to be forgotten. Where once Alice Vesta O'Donnell's experiment was carried out in a family lumber camp, a boy grew happily to manhood. I finish Tom's work thinking of my own childhood, and knowing his last story will not forever remain an uncompleted memory in a box on a shelf.

—William J. O'Hern
February 2012

The North Woods' numerous rivers, and such a combination of natural water power with virgin timber lining its shores, presented an alluring picture to the pioneering O'Donnells.
COURTESY OF CLIFFORD H. GILL FROM *THE MEMORIES OF CLIFFORD D. GILL*

Though devoid of civilization, the former site of the O'Donnell Lumber Camp held memories. The varying greens of the foliage; the russet browns of the camp buildings; wreaths of purple smoke that rose from stove pipes; the light from kerosene lamps that shone through window panes framed by snug log walls; the almost blood-red sunsets, and all the shifting shadows were strong remembrances of past youth. COURTESY OF PAT PAYNE

In the early days, softwood—mainly spruce, hemlock and pine—was lumbered for building purposes. COURTESY OF EARL M. KREUZER

Spruce-tree: Its twigs may be boiled and evaporated into old-fashioned root beer or healing medicines; its lumber is useful and ornamental; its bark roofs the shanties of sportsmen and woodsmen; its the greatest of all as a pulp-producer. COURTESY OF GEORGE SHAUGHNESSY

Near the river, in a small clearing, was a ruined cabin, picturesque in its very desolation. To the O'Donnells, the site was rich in memories. Across the river was a great windfall of more than a half a century ago, marked by soft tamaracks. COURTESY OF CLIFFORD H. GILL FROM *THE MEMOIRS OF CLIFFORD D. GILL*

The former lumber camp settlement has its historic features also. Here are roads long ago abandoned, mere marks, which would show like scars on the tawny earth; in the heydey of lumbering, when this new country had prospects, they were the thoroughfares of widely known industries full of dash and enthusiasm. Just where the children stand, in front of the dining camp, crosses the old road cut during the winder of 1889. Farther down the road is a decayed blacksmith shop, and the spot remains lifeless, like villages whose industries have collapsed. COURTESY OF GEORGE SHAUGHNESSY

High decomposed stumps told of the great snowfall of 1889, when all boundaries were obliterated, and of the cold Friday which followed, when men sat in camp with a fence of blankets behind them, and when water froze almost in the blaze of the fire. COURTESY OF *THE INDEPENDENCE*

Tom O'Donnell enjoyed talking with old timers like Mr. Judson who compared the old and new logging methods. "We'd be up at 2:30 in the morning and work by kerosene torches until it was light. We'd never get a chance to eat from breakfast until dinner. By the end of the season we all looked gaunt and hollow-cheeked. COURTESY OF JOHN DONAHUE

The main floor consisted of two large rooms, a small bedroom, and a pantry. One of the large rooms was used as a kitchen and dining room. The dining area was where paring, heating, and cooking processes were continually going on. The tables were constructed of rough boards and ran the length of the room. All of the men ate at the long tables piled with a rude abundance of food at one time. COURTESY OF MAITLAND C. DESORMO

The typical camp shanty was constructed of spruce logs battened with moss and mud, roofed with hemlock bark and water-proof paper. It had two doors and three windows on the first floor and one window on the second. The men slept on the second-floor room, which consisted of straw ticks, sheets and quilts, and pillows filled with hay, straw or feathers. About three-fourths of the beds were on the floor, the others being rude bedsteads made by the lumberjacks. COURTESY OF LLOYD BLANKMAN

The old bull cooks had a rule of not talking at table. It was rigidly enforced, and a man was given his walking ticket if he abused it. COURTESY OF PAT PAYNE

Judson remembered, "I can recall when a lumber camp was just a small log hut. The doors were very low and they would have around forty men in a camp that had a room for twenty. I can't help but think how we used to pack a big knapsack and walk thirty or forty miles in the mud. When we reached camp, we would go out and break a few boughs and make a bunk. On a stormy day, everyone would come in all wet. The place would be full of old, dirty, wet clothes, and stinking socks, and to top this off, the teamsters would bring in their leather harnesses and drop them on the wood pile. I want you to know that when a good, bit fire got going, the air was not to sanitary." COURTESY OF IRENE E. ROGERS

"We got pretty good meals in the old days, not as fancy—no coffee, fresh fruit, milk or vegetable to speak of—but a man could go for it. I liked it because I wasn't much for pastry and lighter stuff." —George Lanktree. COURTESY OF *THE INDEPENDENCE*

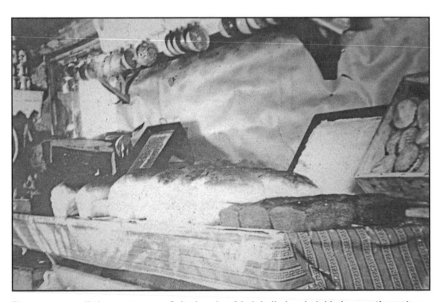

The menu was a little monotonous. Salted pork—fried, boiled and pickled—was the main dish, served along with pots of green and black tea, bread and butter, and potatoes. "I've been in old-time camps all winter and never seen a tablespoon of sugar on the table," George Lanktree swore. COURTESY OF PAT PAYNE

Salt pork was handed out in huge chunks for breakfast, lunch, and dinner, and the day's supply of bread was laid out in a snack in the morning. "When you were hungry," George Lanktree recalled, "it was an A-1 meal, but I guess it wasn't up to the grub today." COURTESY OF PAT PAYNE

The large area called the bull pen served as a recreation room where 'jacks did their mending, told stories, played musical instruments, sang, and played cards and other games. COURTESY OF PAT PAYNE

Jacks would sit puffing their pipes in the evening around the red-hot stove, the set garments steaming and drying, and huddled piles of foot-gear around ... listen to the bandying repartee, the direct pointed humor, the events of the day gone over, the yarns told, the songs sung, the clog-dancing, hear the musician drawing his violin or Jew's harp. COURTESY OF MAITLAND C. DESORMO

In the old days, lumberjacks were for the most part bachelors. COURTESY OF JOHN DONAHUE

In the old days, to the rugged businessmen who lived them, weren't so bad as a lot of people picture them. It was tough going but they liked the life. COURTESY OF JOHN DONAHUE

"A big, healthy'jack was never without a wad of chewing tobacco," George Lanktree told Tom O'Donnell in reliving his life in the early lumber camps with the air of a man who was describing how to separate the men from the boys. COURTESY OF MARILYN BREAKEY

An old lumber camp complex included the smith shop, the barns, the sleeping camp with bunks around three sides, two deep, and, in the middle of the long space a roaring wood-stove. The dining camp was where paring, heating, and cooking processes were continually going on. The long tables were piled with a rude abundance of food. COURTESY OF EARL M. KREUZER

"Winter was cold, deep with snow, and from the beginning the weather was never warm enough to settle the snow." COURTESY OF EARL M. KREUZER

Breaking roads was a demanding task. A stretch of three miles with three and a half feet of snow required three teams of horses breaking through to complete the job in less than two days. COURTESY OF EARL M. KREUZER

A sprinkler-box is being filled at a spring. It sprayed water, turning sled ruts to glare ice and corduroy roads into shining roads. COURTESY OF *THE INDEPENDENCE*

Horses were used to pull the logs to the skidways. COURTESY OF EARL M. KREUZER

The O'Donnell's neighbors lived a rustic pioneer life. COURTESY OF CLIFFORD H. GILL FROM *THE MEMOIRS OF CLIFFORD D. GILL*

Cold decking, an old method, is where logs were heaped in huge piles to be moved out of the woods during spring thaw. COURTESY OF PAT PAYNE

The River Driver is at home on loose logs in running water. He is one of the most picturesque figures in all the lumbering operations. COURTESY OF PAT PAYNE

"Above the Bridge-Dam, the water was covered with floating logs which the Log Drivers were guiding toward the sluice way through which a torrent of water and logs were pouring." —W. B. Downey, Sky Pilot (lumber camp pastor). COURTESY OF MAITLAND C. DESORMO

"At the very moment of my approach to water there appeared to be considerable excitement. A man was desperately riding a log in rough water. To me, it looked as though the man was doomed and yet he was keeping his footing. His fellows were shouting encouragement as they rushed down the banks of the stream on either side to render such help as might be possible." —W. B. Downey. COURTESY OF LAWTON L. WILLIAMS

Tom O'Donnell's own experience at river driving was very limited. He saw much more of it than he participated in. COURTESY OF ED KORNMEYER

"If I knew where I was going to die for sure, I would never go near that place." —Unidentified River Driver. COURTESY OF ED KORNMEYER

"Machines are replacing horses," George Lanktree shared with the staff at *The Northeastern Logger* in 1952. Men are working an eight-hour day. The day's coming when there won't be a horse in camp at all. The time was when a good team was the most important thing a hauler could have. COURTESY OF PAT PAYNE

"I just wonder what some of my old lumberjack pals would say if they could have one peek at the new camps of today," John Carney remembered when he visited *The Northeastern Logger's* office. "They probably would be like the French fellow who went to see a circus for the first time. He saw a giraffe and while he stood there looking it over,he asked one of the circus help what the name of that animal was. The fellow said, 'A giraffe.' The Frenchman said, 'I don't believe there is any such animal.'" COURTESY OF JOHN DONAHUE

Spring mattresses, clean sheets once a week, and freshly-washed blankets were the modern conveniences Lanktree most liked about the new lumber camps. "We used to sleep on board bunks, with spruce or balsam [tips] for mattress. We used the same two pair of double blankets for the whole season. No one bothered with sheets. "Now, a man can have a bath whenever he wants it." he sighed a little wistfully. COURTESY OF MAITLAND C. DESORMO

"The work and the play in the timber camps of the later 19th and early 20th century was a lot simpler than it is today [1952]," said Lanktree. "On an ordinary day, a cutter would go out at dawn and work til dusk. If he felt like it after dinner, he'd play a game of checkers. Otherwise, he would grind his axe and hit the hay." COURTESY OF PAT PAYNE

"The old grey mare ain't what she used to be in the field of lumbering. Gasoline and caterpillar treads have taken her place in the hearts of big-time operators, and motor oil has kicked elbow grease out of top place in the lubrication field." —Mary Ruth White, *Lumber Camp News* reporter. COURTESY OF CARLTON J. SYKES FAMILY

AS SOME of his friends say, it took Tom O'Donnell a long time to find the Black River Country, but when he did, he more than made up for his tardiness. The route that Tom took to the North was longer than Routes 11 or 12 or 365 — or for that matter, longer than all of them together. His roundabout trail led him from the timberlands in the heart of Michigan to New York City, to London, then back to Chicago, Cincinnati, and New York City again.

Finally, after what most people would consider a long, distinguished, and—pardon the expression—completed career, Tom O'Donnell came to Boonville to rest. He remained to write five books—five books that not only have left the stamp of his warm personality on the ancient lands he wrote about, but will be read and read again by others who will come to love the country and to find it, as he found it, forever various and forever new. From now on, loyal readers of *Sapbush Run*, *Snubbing Posts*, *Birth of a River*, *Tip of the Hill*, and *The River Rolls On* may be forgiven

Thomas C. O'Donnell
An Informal History of an Informal Historian

© R.P. Nadeau

LIFE IN A NORTH WOODS LUMBER CAMP

for thinking of a huge portion of the lower Adirondacks as "Tom O'Donnell Country."

Most people who are aware of Tom's vast fund of northern lore naturally think of him as being a native of the land he knows so well. Reviewers of his books and commentators who have turned to him for information refer to him so regularly as "a native of Boonville" that Tom himself thinks nothing of it anymore; he is, in fact, a little proud of having become so much a part of the area which he adopted—or which, as he would put it, adopted him. Not that he has forgotten the other places along the way,

Thomas C. O'Donnell drew on an astonishingly keen memory and told his story accurately of an era long since over in the lumber woods of America's Northern Forest.

nor the host of friends he acquired during his years as a busy editor and writer. Tom has a fine, sharp memory, and it's a good thing, because with so much work to do these days, that memory is as busy as the Black River itself. His memory has its headwaters—to use a term of which Tom would approve—in Michigan.

In the heavily wooded northeastern corner of Montcalm County, about as close to the heart of Michigan's Lower Peninsula as you can get, lies Vestaburg. There, in the settlement that Tom's father had founded and named for his wife, Tom was born in a year which his friends do not discuss for the simple reason that no one thinks of him in terms of age. Vestaburg, Tom remembers, was a good place for a boy to get started in life. To the north and east flows the Pine River; farther up, in Midland County, where Tom was to do most of his growing up, is the Salt River. And all through the territory were dozens of the little creeks and brooks that can be so fascinating to a boy. Through all his early years Tom was to live close to one or another of the many logging streams that cut across the peninsula toward Saginaw and the lumber market. Tom has commented frequently on the part that rivers have seemed to play in his life—rivers, and timber, and the men who cut and float the timber.

Born into a logging community, Tom had to learn its ways early. Oldtimers in Forestport and Lyons Falls will be glad—but probably not surprised—to learn that he owned his own peavey when he was six, and that he had lived through his first inglorious ducking before he was seven. Most of the learning was pleasant, as it can be for a boy who has plenty of trees and rivers around, and some of it was permanent. He acquired, from watching the skilled woodsmen, a love of good workmanship. "I loved a woodsman who in notching a tree could cut a clean, true V in the bole," he has said. "Or a sawyer, or a pair of them, who in sawing off a log could swing with the saw so that on a pull through the log it was cutting every inch of the way." This kind of proficiency he deliberately cultivated and applied later to his own work of writing and editing.

Many years afterward, while wandering with aim and delight from Westernville to North Lake, from Little Falls to Lowville, always gathering anecdotes for his books, Tom was grateful for his Michigan boyhood. Men who have lived with nature talk to one another easily, and Tom had no trouble communicating with those whose business was with trees and rivers. All through his books the reader can feel the native kinship with men who work their way through forests. Venerable railroaders passed on to him stories about the old Black River and Utica Railroad—the "Sapbush Run" of northern tradition; old canallers found him an eager audience for their yarns about brawls along the Black River Canal; old guides, woodsmen, and hunters in the Black River headwaters country recalled for him the fabled exploits of Atwell Martin and Dingle Dangle Jones, and read about themselves in *Birth of a River*. All of this, perhaps, because Michigan's Montcalm and Midland Counties are not so very unlike New York's Lewis, Herkimer, and Oneida Counties—filled with streams and forests, and best of all with friendly people conscious of their own colorful past.

Like the woodsmen he admired, Tom O'Donnell learned his craft carefully and he learned it well. The years between 1904, when he was in London, and 1943, when he came to Boonville, are an amazing record of enough editorial and literary experiences to fill half a dozen ordinary biographies. As a young assistant editor in England, for instance (he had gone to London originally as a secretary to a clergyman-uncle), he delighted in rambling through Wordsworth's Lake District, in climbing through craggy Welsh mountain ranges, in sitting in the gallery of the British House of Commons and hearing the great and the near-great discuss Europe's destiny. Asquith, Lloyd-George, Austen Chamberlain were men of power in England then, and young Tom saw and listened to them often. He heard another great leader—Tim Healy, "the glorious Irishman"—address the Commons in pure classic Greek. And he listened carefully to the admirable diction of a young statesman named Winston Churchill as he made his first speech as a member of the new Liberal government. Then, always striving for precision and clarity in his own writing, Tom studied classic models. His favorite pastime in those days was reading the Greek New Testament, his choice as the ultimate in precision and clarity and majestic beauty.

After five wonderful years in England, Tom returned to America as managing editor of *Good Health Magazine*. He took with him to Michigan—this time to Battle Creek—his lovely bride, who had been Bertha Smith, of Bellefontaine, Ohio, and who shares Tom's career today as completely as she did in the earlier stages.

Tom's vigor as an editor prompted Battle Creek College, a school that liked new ideas, to invite him to introduce some of his theories about composition into the classroom. His teaching was so successful that he might have continued there for years, had not the time come for him to move up and along. In 1918, he went to Chicago, which for a decade had been rivaling New York City as a literary and publishing center. In Chicago, Tom edited cartoons, conducted courses in various aspects of writing, and made more friends.

Chicago in 1918 was a mecca for writers and artists who had already achieved recognition or were about to achieve it. Among Tom's friends there was Carl Sandburg, then an editorial writer for the *Chicago Daily News*. Sandburg's *Cornhuskers* was about to be published, and he and Tom could talk about its prospects over lunch, or as they wandered through the secondhand bookstores. There was Vincent Starrett, too, the great scholar-author who founded "The Baker Street Irregulars," the fabulous society dedicated to the worship of Sherlock Holmes; there was Bert Leston Taylor, the first of the great daily newspaper columnists; there were the McCutcheon brothers—George, whose novels (*Graustark* and *Brewster's Millions* among them) were to sell more than five million copies, and John, the great cartoonist who was to win the Pulitzer Prize for his work in 1931; and there was Edgar Rice Burroughs, who had created *Tarzan* in 1914. Tom O'Donnell knew them all, and worked with them all. And to this day he admires them all as good workmen, each in his own way, who could cut a "clean, true V in the bole."

In Chicago, too, Tom could seek out and encourage worthy young talent. Among those he helped in his editorial capacity was John Van Alstyne Weaver, a young Hamilton College graduate who was writing his free verse in Chicago. He helped a cartoonist named Seager who had an idea for a comic strip, but needed assistance in getting it on the market. The strip was about a strange sailor named "Popeye."

Meanwhile, Tom had been busy with his own writing, too. Already he had two books to his credit—*The Family Food* had been published in 1912 and *The Healthful House* in 1916. Both books had been produced in connection with his duties with *Good Health Magazine* and Battle Creek College. He had fun writing them, to be sure, and they had been successful. But neither brought him the fun and success that came with *The Ladder of Rickety Rungs*, which came out in 1923. Somewhere within a stone's throw of anyone reading these words there are at least two or three young adults who, as children, read and loved this minor classic of children's literature. Beautifully illustrated by Janet Laura Scott, and with a preface by Padraic Colum, the great Irish author, *The Ladder of Rickety Rungs* sold 30,000 copies in its first edition and is still a popular item in the children's room in most public libraries. Tom remembers this book with special fondness, as well he might: Reading it became part of the growing process for a whole generation of Americans.

In 1922 Tom moved on again, to Cincinnati and a post with *The Writer's Digest*, the professional writer's trade journal. In Cincinnati, in addition to his editorial duties, he wrote and produced on Station WLW a series of plays for children. This little job made him a pioneer in still another field, since only one other radio station in America had tried it earlier. Some of the plays were published and subsequently produced time and again. One of them, "The Sandman's Brother," is included in a widely-used anthology of children's plays.

After five happy and fruitful years in Cincinnati, Tom was called in 1927 to his most important job yet. The Masonic Outlook, which the Grand Lodge of Masons had recently founded in New York City as a monthly periodical, was in need of a hustling managing editor. Tom took over the job, planning to combine his beloved freelance writing with his editorial chores. In a short time, however, the ailing editor-in-chief of the Outlook retired, leaving Tom in full command. Since the magazine had a circulation of about 15,000, its new editor didn't have as much time as he would have liked for freelancing. He made time, nevertheless, for something he had always loved to do, children's verse. *Child Life*, the first of the great children's magazines in every sense, was always waiting for Tom's delightful jingles, and from that magazine many of them were reprinted in children's anthologies and readers. One of them, especially, has been so widely reprinted that even Tom has to remind himself that he wrote it. That's the one about the pink giraffe:

> *The pink giraffe lives in a tree—*
> *The upper part, I mean;*
> *His legs are down with you and me,*
> *The rest is in between.*

There were others, too, many others that he wrote for his own children and for all children.

As a lover of great stories told in simple language, Tom had long been eager to render some of the classics into English so simple that even four- and six-year-olds could understand and appreciate the stories. Accordingly, in 1936 he wrote a rendition of the Old Testament especially designed to capture the imagination and appreciation of children. This little book, published by the Gettinger Press, was so enthusiastically received by all religious denominations that Tom followed it up with similar renditions of The Lord's Prayer and The Bill of Rights. Today, eighteen years after their publication, Tom has a special place in his heart for these little books. They best embody, as he puts it, his love for simplicity of language—the kind of simplicity that lends such power to the Gospel of St. John, to the Greek classics, and to the Psalms of David.

Meanwhile, his job as editor of *The Masonic Outlook* happily required frequent trips to Boonville, where the magazine was printed. These trips led to regular summer sojourns at Long Lake, where Tom found "opportunity to learn and love the country and to become acquainted with so many estimable people." Then too, it was good to be back in a region where lumbering was as important as it had been in his boyhood country in Michigan. So, after a spell of illness in 1943, Tom naturally turned to the Black River Country for rest and content. The hills and valleys—and the river itself, which winds through his books even when it doesn't seem to be invited—were what he needed.

Unfortunately for his original plan, however, Tom O'Donnell had overlooked one thing: He had never learned to rest. Soon his capacity as a good listener and his native curiosity about persons and places betrayed him. The stories that he inevitably heard as he wandered in his amiable fashion from place to place—the countless touches of tradition and legend that are casually heard and soon forgotten by the average person—began to make an impression on him. These North Country people, he found, were acutely aware of their past, and were eager to hear more about it. Tom wrote a series of sketches for the *Boonville Herald*; they were so well received that it was natural for him to start thinking in terms of books. Before long, the thought of rest and retirement was forgotten, and the battered O'Donnell typewriter was busier than ever. There were books to be written, books for his friends—"the lumberjacks, farmers, small people on the back, dirt roads." Books that they could read and enjoy and read again. That these friends read and appreciated the books is shown not alone by their sales, but by the countless letters and friendly comments that Tom treasures with the rest of his flood of memories.

Tom O'Donnell moved along again in 1953—this time to Winter Park, Florida, a town that years ago lured another North Country writer, Irving Bacheller. Before he left, one of his friends asked him seriously how many books he planned to write during this retirement. Others wonder how long it will be before the hills and valleys—and always that river—call him back. Whether or not he plans to return, however, his readers can be sure that he's busy, always gathering more anecdotes and meeting more "estimable people." He will always meet them, wherever he goes.

—Thomas F. O'Donnell, 1954

Glossary of Basic Terms

Birling—spinning a log in the water by running on it, without falling off.

Block and tackle—a wooden block with a wooden pulley inside; a rope runs through the pulley and hooks to a log or sleigh or whatever had to be.

Bootjack—a wooden board with a rounded notch to pull boots off. The bootjack would have a small piece of wood (1" x 2") crossways on the bottom to elevate it on the end that had the rounded part on it.

(Spring) break up—when the frost came out of the log hauling roads and the ice broke up in the rivers at the end of winter.

Broad axe—has a ten-inch cutting edge and a curved wooden handle. A hewer would stand straddling the log or side of the log, then take a chalk line to mark where he wanted to cut along the length of the log, turning the log until all four sides were done.

Bull of the woods—the foreman of the logging camp.

Bull puncher—a logger who skids logs out of the woods using oxen.

Calked boots—leather boots with half-inch calks (pronounced "corks") in them. They had a screw thread on one end and a pointed end (like a nail) on the other end. It took a specific tool to place them in the soles of boots.

Calks—pronounced "corks," the nails that went into calked boots.

Cant hook—lacks a spike on the end like a peavey. Instead, it has a hook to turn a log in the mill after it has been squared up. That log is called a cant at that point.

Chopper—a logger who cuts trees down.

Cooper—a person who makes barrels.

Crib—twenty or more logs lashed together to form a small raft.

Cruising timber—when the forester walks through a piece of woods to estimate how much timber is there and its value.

Dray—A woods "dray" consisted of two runners held together by a bunk halfway back from the front end, where a "nose" with a hole through the chain is attached to the bunk, and wrapped around the log to hold it in place.

Felling—the act of cutting a tree down.

Finishing mill—a sawmill that produced smooth wood.

Forester—his job is cruising the timber.

Hewer—a logger who squared timber.

Logmanship—ability to select the best cut out of a tree to get what logs out of it.

Milldam—a dam built to hold back water to make a millpond.

Millpond—the widened river behind the milldam.

Notcher—a lumberjack who cuts a wedge shape out of the tree trunk to make the tree fall in the intended direction.

Peavey—a four-foot wooden handle with an iron hook on the bottom and a pointed spike at the end.

Peeling—when the bark is peeled off spruce and hemlock in April, May and June.

Pike pole—a wooden handle about ten feet long which has an iron screw tip with a small hook on the side of it; used in the river drives.

River driver—a logger who keeps logs moving down the river to the sawmill.

River landing—location where logs are piled on the frozen surface of a river.

Road monkey—a man who took care of the skid roads during the winter season.

Rollway—a pile of logs waiting by the river waiting for the spring ice breakup.

Sawyer—a person who runs the saw to cut wood in a sawmill.

Scaler—the man who figures how much footage is in a log.

Skid—to haul logs out of the woods.

Skidway—a pile of logs waiting in the woods to be loaded.

Shanty camp—a log or board building in the woods where loggers ate and slept.

Sky pilot—ministers who went from camp to camp to preach the Christian faith.

Sleigh—has two or four runners with two wooden cross pieces to pile the logs on; towed by horses or tractors in the winter.

Snaked out—seven or eight logs chained together end-to-end to be pulled out of the woods by horse or tractor.

Swale—a wet spot in the woods.

Teamster—a logger who hauls logs from the skidway to the river.

Tote road—a road that is used to bring supplies into the logging camp.

Tote team—team of horses.

Turkey—a fabric satchel attached to the end of a short pole used to hold personal items. Carried slung over one's shoulder.

Acknowledgements

The primary documents comprising this book are the Thomas Clay O'Donnell Papers, Special Collections Research Center, Syracuse University Library, Syracuse, New York.

Thomas C. O'Donnell's historical and warm human-interest story would not have been possible without the support of the Special Collections Research Center at Syracuse University Library and that of his grandson, Thomas A. O'Donnell. With respect to their generosity, I feel especially fortunate.

Writing projects require the backing of many skilled people. For their assistance in helping me in the production of Thomas C. O'Donnell's unrefined draft I am indebted to Nicolette A. Dobrowolski, Head of Public Services Reference and Access Services Librarian, Special Collections Research Center, Syracuse University Library; my daughters Susan Steverman and Kerry Suppa, who typed the manuscript; Rob Igoe, Jr. publisher of North Country Books; Roy Reehil publisher of The Forager Press; and the owners of some very old and consequently greatly prized pictures.

Mary L. Dennis and Neal S. Burdick were rough and final editors of this project. Their knowledge, insight and instincts were instrumental in enhancing the book's readability.

The book and cover design and typesetting were created by Nancy Did It! (www.NancyDidIt.com)

For permission to use vintage logging photos from their personal collections, recognition goes to Marilyn Breakey; George R. Cataldo; Clifford H. Gill; John Donahue; Eric Johnson, Executive Editor at *The Northern Logger* published by the Northeastern Loggers Association in Old Forge,

N.Y.; Leigh Portner; Irene E. Rogers; Town of Webb Historical Society; Dorothy Payton; and Paul Sykes.

I would also like to acknowledge, posthumously, Lloyd Blankman; G. Glyndon Cole, editor and publisher of *North Country Life* and *York State Tradition* magazines; Maitland C. DeSormo; Edward Kornmeyer; Earl M. Kreuzer; Winfred Murdock; Pat Payne; George Shaughnessy; and Lawton L. Williams

Grateful acknowledgement is made to Richard Nadeau who created the "River Driver" illustration used on the chapter title pages, and granted permission for its use. "River Driver" products are available at Moose River Trading Co. in Thendara, NY (www.mooserivertrading.com)

Grateful acknowledgement is also made to Sheri Amsel for her drawings that end each chapter.

I have made every effort to acknowledge the assistance of everyone who helped with this project; any omission is an unintentional oversight.

Bibliography

Interviews
Thomas A. O'Donnell, interviews with William J. O'Hern,
July and August 2010.

Books
Bird, Barbara Kephart. *Calked Shoes, Life in Adirondack Lumber Camps.*
Prospect, NY: Prospect Books, 1952.

Reed, Frank A. *Lumberjack Sky Pilot.* Old Forge, NY:
North Country Books, 1965.

Magazines
Unknown author. "In an Adirondack Lumber Camp."
The Outlook, Jan. 4, 1902.

O'Donnell, Thomas C. "Readin' and Writin.'" *The Northeastern
Logger.* Old Forge, NY: The Northeasten Logger, February, 1952.

Unknown author. "Cribbed from Contemporaries." *The Northeastern
Logger.* Old Forge, NY: The Northeasten Logger, November, 1952.

Unknown author. "Readin' and Writin.'" *The Northeastern Logger.*
Old Forge, NY: The Northeasten Logger, December, 1952.

O'Donnell, Thomas F. "Thomas C. O'Donnell, An Informal History
of an Informal Historian." *North Country Life*, Fall 1954.

Manuscripts
Thomas Clay O'Donnell Papers, Special Collections Research Center,
Syracuse University Library.

Newspapers

Unknown author. "Unknown title." *The Lumber Camp News*, December, 1950.

White, Mary Ruth. "Tughill Lumbering—Old and New." *The Lumber Camp News*, June, 1950.

Unknown author. "Tughill Lumberine—Old and New" *The Lumber Camp News*, June, 1950.

"Old-time Bushworker Recalls Life in Logging Camps." *The Northeastern Logger*, December, 1952.

Unknown author. "Canal Films to be Shown in Lowville: Towpath Color Film Received Wide Praise Here." *Boonville Herald*, October 1, 1952.

Unknown author. "First Volume of Trilogy on Black River Published Oct. 15." *The Journal and Republican*, September 2, 1952.

Unknown author. "Famous Neighbors: Thomas C. O'Donnell Has Encouraged Young Writers in His Long Magazine Career." [Date unknown].

Unknown author. "What Happened Here Once." Utica *Observer-Dispatch*, November 22, 1952.

Unknown author. "Fairfield Seminary Latest Theme of Boonville Author." *Herkimer Evening Telegram*, June 10, 1951.

Unknown author. "Log Drives, Hermits, Guides Feature 'Informal History.'" *Herkimer Evening Telegram*, October, 1953.

Arthur, Phyllis-Marie. "Birth of a River Tells Tall Stories of Black River." *The Journal and Republican*, October 23, 1952.

Bird, Barbara K. "Birth of a River." *North Country Life*, Fall 1952.

Cain, Cliff. "Boonville Author's Book Highlights Personalities of Black River Source." *Rome Sentinel*, October 18, 1952.

Merrill, Arch. "Black River Book Third of Kind." *Rochester Democrat and Chronicle*, November 16, 1952.

Nuisser, Clayton A. "Spirit of Early North Country Days Recalled in New Black River Book." *Boonville Herald*, October 16, 1952.

Spears, E. A. "Boonville Man Pens Informal, Rich History of Black River." Utica *Observer-Dispatch*, [date unknown].

Williams, J. Robert. "Black River Source Described in Book." *Watertown Times*, October 21, 1952.

Index

Upcoming releases by
William J. O'Hern

Adirondack Pastimes:
Camping and Sporting Adventures in the Cold River (1913–1950)
with Jay L. Gregory, C.V. Latimer, M.D. and Noah John Rondeau

Discovering the Memoirs of Emily Wires (1885–1975):
A Window into the Old Days of the Adirondacks

Adirondack Wilds:
Exploring the Haunts of Noah John Rondeau

Adirondack Kaleidoscope
and North Country Characters

Adirondack Memories

Gathered Memories Vol. I

Gathered Memories Vol. II

Logging in the Adirondacks:
The Revolutionary Linn Tractor and Lumber Camp Stories

Adirondack Echoes:
A Portrait of Camp Life a Century Ago

The Informal History of the Moose River Plains

Remembering Noah John Rondeau:
Following an Adirondack Hermit's Footsteps through His Final Years

View Previews of Future Releases
by William J. O'Hern at www.adkwilds.com